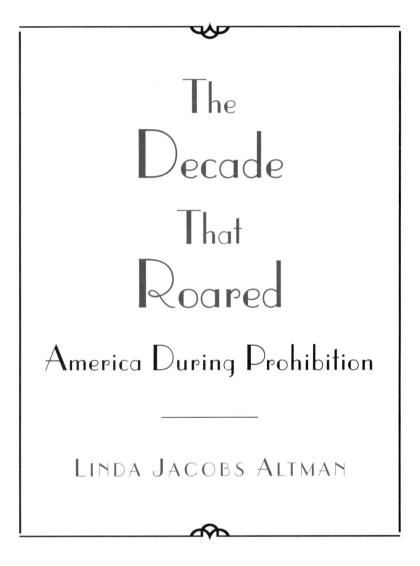

The
Decade
That
Roared

America During Prohibition

LINDA JACOBS ALTMAN

Twenty-First Century Books
A Division of Henry Holt and Company | New York

Twenty-First Century Books
A Division of Henry Holt and Company, Inc.
115 West 18th Street
New York, NY 10011

Henry Holt® and colophon are trademarks of
Henry Holt and Company, Inc.
Publishers since 1866

Library of Congress Cataloging-in-Publication Data

Altman, Linda Jacobs, 1943–
The decade that roared: America during prohibition/Linda Jacobs Altman.
p. cm.
Includes bibliographical references and index.
Summary: Discusses the social conditions of the decade during
which prohibition was in effect, the results of the legislation,
and its failure to preserve traditional values.
1. United States—History—1919–1933—Juvenile literature.
2. United States—Social life and customs—1918–1945—
Juvenile literature. 3. United States—Social conditions—1918–1932—
Juvenile literature. Prohibition—United States—History—20th century—
Juvenile literature. [1. United States—History—1919–1933. 2. United
States—Social life and customs—1918–1945. 3. United States—
Social Conditions—1918–1932. 4. Prohibition.] I Title.
E784.A65
973.91'dc21   97-8727
                                                                        CIP
                                                                        AC

ISBN 0-8050-4133-8

Designed by Kelly Soong

Printed in the United States of America
All first editions are printed on acid-free paper ∞.

1 3 5 7 9 10 8 6 4 2

For the real Palmer girls,
in loving memory.

CONTENTS

INTRODUCTION

From its beginning in 1920 to its end in 1933, prohibition shaped and defined the decade that historians have called "The Roaring Twenties." It was a time of transition, when the frontier no longer beckoned, the Great War was over, and America had plunged into what F. Scott Fitzgerald, author of the definitive twenties novel *The Great Gatsby*, would describe as "the greatest, gaudiest spree in history."[1]

In the cities and college towns all across the country young people seemed reckless, wild, endlessly hungry for new experiences. Population patterns shifted as thousands left small towns and family farms for the faster pace of city living. The moral certainties of the small-town Protestant ethic gave way to the endless uncertainties of a secular, scientific era that generated more questions than answers.

Changes piled one on top of the other, reaching into every area of life. Albert Einstein's special theory of relativity had been around since 1905; in the twenties, it began to supplant both the earlier physics of Sir Isaac Newton and the biblical account of divine creation. Charles Darwin's *Origin of Species* (published 1859) and *The Descent of Man* (1871) gained widespread acceptance in the twenties, gradually replacing the biblical *Genesis* as the preferred explanation for human origins.

Applied technology also accounted for a good part of the "roar" in the Roaring Twenties. The automobile was a novelty in 1908 when Henry Ford produced the first Model T; it became a necessity for the newly mobile lifestyle of the twenties. The first regularly scheduled radio broadcasts occurred in 1920; by 1924 America had coast-to-coast hookups. Motion pictures came of age as stars like Charlie Chaplin and Mary Pickford transformed a sleepy farming town called Hollywood into the glittering "movie capital of the world." These new media reached people in Portland, Maine, and Portland, Oregon, with the same news and entertainment; the result was the birth of "mass culture."

The Eighteenth Amendment establishing prohibition wasn't the only far-reaching change to the Constitution: the Nineteenth Amendment gave women the right to vote. Thousands of women exercised that new right in the presidential election of 1920, helping to send Warren G. Harding to the White House.

Framed and shaped by all these forces, the Roaring Twenties could be described as a decade of extremes. It produced the first African-American labor union (the Brotherhood of Pullman Porters) and an unnerving revival of the Ku Klux Klan; the flamboyant speakeasy queen "Texas" Guinan and the equally flamboyant evangelist Aimee Semple McPherson; the ruthless gangster Al Capone and the gentleman rumrunner Bill McCoy. For many Americans, breaking the law seemed to become not only permissible but fashionable, as thousands risked arrest to drink, dance, and hobnob with high rollers, movie stars, and millionaires.

As the only constitutional amendment ever to be repealed, prohibition was not simply a failure—it was a spectacular failure. It began as a last, desperate effort to preserve traditional values against urbanization, industrialization, and that hazy evil known as "modernism." It ended by threatening the very traditions it was meant to protect.

ONE

DOING AWAY WITH "DEMON RUM"
The Temperance Crusade Against Alcohol

A large, hard-eyed woman burst into a noisy saloon, brandishing an axe. A troop of militant women followed at her heels. "Smash, women, smash!" she commanded. Whereupon the demonstrators proceeded to destroy as much of the place as they could before somebody figured out how to stop them.

At 175 pounds and around six feet tall, Carry Nation was as formidable as she was relentless. Saloon keepers trembled at the mention of her name. She was the most audacious leader of the early prohibition crusade; an avenging angel who blamed "demon rum" for the untimely death of her alcoholic husband.

Carry had a score to settle, and she was not about to be timid in her methods. Though she died on June 11, 1911, almost a decade before prohibition became law, the big woman armed with an axe and her own moral outrage came to personify the temperance crusade.

"THE BEER COSTS A NICKEL; THE FOOD IS FREE"

As the transcontinental railroad crossed the country in the 1860s, saloons went along for the ride. Railroad construction began in 1863 from the east and 1865 from the west. It ended on May 10, 1869, when the two lines joined at Promontory Point, Utah. Along the way, saloons were a regular feature of the "tent cities" that followed the work camps. They offered everything from laundry services and shoe repair to gambling, prostitution, and generous quantities of whiskey and beer.

Some of these portable towns packed up and left when the work crews moved on. Others turned into rough-and-ready frontier settlements, with clapboard buildings and rutted dirt roads. The heart and soul of every main street was the local saloon. It was not just a place to get a drink—it was an unofficial community center for workingmen who had no place else to go. For a single nickel, the price of a beer, a man could have music, dancing, and constant conversation. He could always find a card game if he was in the mood for gambling, a warm fire if he was cold, or a washroom if he was tired and dirty from a long day's work.

By far the most important contribution of the saloon to working-class life was the free lunch. Many a worker could not have afforded to live without these daily spreads of crackers, cheese, and sandwiches. There was, of course, an elaborate if unspoken protocol regarding food and liquor; bartenders and bouncers became expert at spotting freeloaders who were ill-mannered enough to eat more than they drank.

COMING TO AMERICA

Around the turn of the century, the United States experienced a floodtide of immigration from southern and eastern Europe. These new arrivals shared neither the Protestant religion nor the Puritanical social codes of much of mainstream America. They were Jews, Catholics, and Eastern Orthodox Christians: "people generally grouped as 'Slavs' and 'Latins' and sniffed at in suspicion and disdain," according to Bernard Weisberger in an article for *American Heritage* magazine.[1]

For the most part, immigrants did not receive a friendly welcome from a public that doubted their ability to adapt to American ways. According to Weisberger, many native-born Americans scorned Italians as "uncivilized," Poles as "stupid," and eastern European Jews as "embarrassing" with their beards, side curls, and skullcaps.[2]

This unreasoning bigotry put up a barrier that the immigrants could not easily cross. Set apart by language, culture, and grinding poverty, they often crowded together in grim, disease-infested tenements. The saloon followed them into most slums, becoming a place of refuge, where a workingman could forget his troubles, drink with people who understood his language, and pretend that all was well. Unfortunately, this pretending sometimes involved public drunkenness and rowdy behavior that offended the sensibilities of so-called polite society.

RALLYING 'ROUND THE CAUSE

Saloons made ideal targets for would-be moral reformers. They tended to be grimy, noisy, and disreputable, with the stench of sweat and beer and cheap cigars hanging in the air. As dens of iniquity (wickedness, sin) they had no equal; prostitution flourished, bar brawls ended in murder, and fathers drank and gambled while their families went hungry. Workers became less efficient and more accident prone after their saloon lunches.

The Women's Christian Temperance Union (WCTU) and the Anti-Saloon League (ASL) led the fight against alcoholic beverages in general and saloons in particular. The WCTU was founded in 1874 by activist women whose goals went beyond prohibition to include prison reform, child labor laws, and most especially women's suffrage. By 1914, the WCTU had focused exclusively on the temperance movement, though many of its members remained active in the suffrage movement.

The Anti-Saloon League was a political action group made

up of well-to-do businessmen who were not above using their wealth and personal influence to advance the cause of prohibition. Their leader, Wayne B. Wheeler, has been called "the most effective lobbyist in American history."[3] He was a small, balding man with a pencil moustache and a thoroughly forgettable face, yet he was a master strategist and promoter.

Wheeler found support for prohibition in the Fundamentalist churches and small towns of America's heartland. He formed alliances with churches and civic groups in order to push through state and local prohibition laws. By 1914, twenty-three states and an unknown number of municipalities had banned liquor and gone dry, at least on paper. Most of them made no effort to stop people from buying liquor elsewhere, for use in their own homes. Many tolerated the sale of beer and wine, only enforcing the law against "hard liquor"—distilled spirits like whiskey, vodka, and gin.

These dry jurisdictions became living laboratories for Anti-Saloon researchers eager to prove their point about the evils of booze. For example, in the year after Battle Creek, Michigan, became a dry town, 420 people went to jail, costing the taxpayers $7,560. The year before, when saloons still flourished, 1,116 people had ended up in jail at a cost of more than $20,000.[4] With dollars-and-cents statistics like that, the ASL was able to enlist the support of industrial barons, such as the redoubtable Henry Ford of Model-T fame, in their cause. Other businessmen soon joined Ford in the crusade for an alcohol-free workplace.

Many employers used outrageously high-handed tactics to enforce company rules against drinking. Ford himself sent representatives into workers' homes to find out about their drinking habits. The REO Motor Car Company of Lansing, Michigan, used private detectives to identify workers who drank, smoked, or voted against prohibition. These company investigators were not above using whatever means were necessary to expose intemperance and to punish offenders with public humiliation, docks (reductions) in their pay, or even outright loss of their jobs.

In their zeal to oppose demon rum, temperance activists were willing to use scare tactics, threatening debility, despair, and eternal damnation for those intemperate souls who polluted their bodies with alcohol. In their condemnation of intoxicating beverages, the crusaders did not distinguish between moderate drinking and alcohol abuse. Total abstinence was their goal, and they preached it with all the persuasiveness at their command.

The WCTU prayed and preached and sang. In meetings reminiscent of old-time tent revivals, they celebrated abstinence, decried the use of all intoxicants, and stirred audiences to tears with sentimental hymns about the evils of drink. Their favorite songs had titles like "Under the Curse," "Breaking Mother's Heart," "The Drunkard's Lament," and "Father, Dear Father Come Home."

At the end of each rally, the WCTU passed out printed cards and prevailed upon the audience to sign their names, change their lives, and "take the pledge" that would put them on the side of right and virtue: "I hereby solemnly promise, GOD HELPING ME, to abstain from all distilled, fermented and malt liquors, including wine, beer and cider; and to employ all proper means to discourage the use of, and traffic in the same."[5]

A CRISIS OF CONSCIENCE

During the decade that began with 1910, change came fast and furious; far faster than most people's ability to assimilate it. War, revolution, and social upheaval paved the way into the turmoil of the decade that roared. World War I (also called "the Great War") began in 1914, plunging most of Europe into armed conflict. This was a different kind of warfare, fought with new and unthinkable weaponry: machine guns, armored tanks, poison gas, and flame throwers. For the first time in history, airplanes soared over the battlefields, bombing enemy ground forces, and "dog-fighting" (engaging in aerial combat) with enemy planes.

During the pivotal year of 1917, old alliances crumbled and new ones came into being. In June, the United States entered the Great War, fighting with the "Allies" (France, Great Britain, and Russia) against the "Central Powers" (Germany, Austria-Hungary, and Turkey). In October, the communist revolution deposed Czar (Emperor) Nicholas II from the throne of Russia, and the Soviet Union came into being. Its leaders made a separate peace with the Central Powers and withdrew from the conflict in Europe to tend to matters at home.

The fighting lasted for another year. On November 11, 1918, the Central Powers surrendered to the Allies and agreed to the armistice (truce, or temporary peace agreement) that brought an end to the fighting. The formal treaty followed in June 1919.

On the brink of a new decade, war and revolution had transformed the world. In the tanks and airplanes of the Great War, Americans had seen a new and deadly kind of warfare. In communism, they saw a new threat to democracy and individual liberty. Against this backdrop of political and social upheaval, thousands longed for an older, simpler time when life seemed predictable, moral codes absolute, and people more sure of their place in the scheme of things.

It was during this crisis of conscience that Congress passed the Eighteenth Amendment, prohibiting "the manufacture, sale, or transportation of intoxicating liquors." The amendment was quickly ratified by the necessary two thirds majority of states, and on January 16, 1919, it became part of the Constitution.

NEW DAY DAWNING

Supporters of prohibition predicted wonderful things as a result of the passage of the Eighteenth Amendment. "When the laboring man works eight hours and spends none of his time at the saloon," wrote William Allen White, editor of the Emporia (Kansas) *Gazette*, "he will save up more money and better his economic status. This will lift more and more men from the laboring class to the economic middle class. . . ."[6]

Though the Eighteenth Amendment had made prohibition the law of the land, it did not provide for enforcement of that prohibition. That task fell to a piece of legislation known as the Volstead Act, which Congress passed in October 1919, more than nine months after the Eighteenth Amendment was ratified by the states.

The Volstead Act was scheduled to go into force at midnight on January 16, 1920. Because it allowed private individuals to keep and use alcoholic beverages obtained before that deadline, thousands of people descended on the existing liquor supply like sharks in a feeding frenzy, buying everything they could find.

As "the good stuff" disappeared into basements and wine cellars, some adventuresome souls went to extreme measures to get one last drink before the Volstead Act went into effect. At one Christmas party in Connecticut, enterprising guests made up for the lack of champagne by toasting the season with toxic wood (rubbing) alcohol. That night, more than seventy people died and dozens more were blinded; hardly an auspicious beginning for a law that was supposed to save society from demon rum and the people from themselves. Prohibitionists wrote off the Connecticut incident as an isolated problem.

On the night of January 16, supporters of prohibition gathered in churches all over America to pray and sing hymns and keep watch until midnight, when the "noble experiment," as prohibition came to be called, was set to begin. At the stroke of twelve, bells pealed forth in joyous celebration as earnest prohibitionists hailed a new era of clean living, family harmony, and economic prosperity.

Not everyone joined the celebration. Before the bells had

quit ringing, would-be bootleggers were making plans to sell liquor and unrepentant drinkers were making plans to buy it. Sportswriter Ring Lardner, who was known for sardonic wit and a generally gloomy outlook on life, penned a tongue-in-cheek obituary for legal liquor:

> Goodbye forever to my old friend booze.
> Dog-gone, I've got the prohibition blues.[7]

TWO

LAW AND DISORDER
Trying to Enforce Prohibition

Breaking the law, or at least bending it severely, seemed to become America's favorite pastime as many ordinary, law-abiding folk flaunted prohibition with a wink and a smile. Like banned books and scandalous gossip, alcoholic beverages became irresistibly attractive for the simple reason that they were forbidden.

At times it seemed as if everybody was getting into the act. By 1926, respectable citizens were "going public." *Time* magazine published a recipe for making gin in its November 22 issue. The wife of the Speaker of the House of Representatives admitted to having "a small still" in her home, and New York City mayor Fiorello La Guardia gave a beer-making demonstration for dozens of reporters at a press conference. In a San Francisco bootlegging trial, the entire jury was arrested for drinking up the evidence while it was supposed to be deliberating the verdict.

LEGAL LOOPHOLES

The Volstead Act allowed individuals to make "nonintoxicating" (defined as containing less than 0.5 percent alcohol) cider and fruit juices for home use. Businesses could manufacture and sell *denatured* (made unfit for consumption) industrial alcohol to paint companies and other legitimate enterprises. They could also produce alcoholic beverages for medicinal and sacramental purposes. People who did not wish to become teetotalers (non-drinkers) became adept at devising technically legal ways to obtain alcoholic beverages.

The easiest and most obvious dodge was "medicinal" use. Cough syrups made with alcohol as the principal ingredient became exceptionally popular for every cold, cough, and sniffle. Doctors prescribed rum toddies for sore throats, spiced wine for digestive problems, and whiskey for nervous tension. Before long, prescriptions for medicinal alcohol accounted for a million gallons per year, all of it legal.[1]

Wine was easy to produce within the letter of the law. One enterprising vintner created "wine bricks"—grape juice concentrated down to solid cubes, about the size of a pound of butter. Careful instructions told the purchaser exactly how to "prevent" the reconstituted juice from fermenting into wine—which would, of course, be quite illegal. Another favorite dodge came from California, where wineries that would otherwise have been idle produced Vine-Glo, a legal product that would turn into wine if stored in a cellar for sixty days. As with the bricks, Vine-Glo came with explicit instructions for "preventing" fermentation.

Beer was somewhat more difficult to manage because there was no way to pass off the basic ingredients as fruit juice. Established breweries tried to survive by producing near-beer, which contained less than the legal limit of 0.5 percent alcohol. Unfortunately, the taste of this weakened brew left a great deal to be desired, and sales were disappointingly poor. Finally, someone hit on the solution: half-brewed beer, called *wort*, contained no alcohol at all. By selling it along with a package of yeast to complete the brewing process (supposedly up to but not exceeding the 0.5 percent legal limit, of course) brewers outfoxed the law and managed to stay in business throughout the "dry" twenties.

Not only did breweries and wineries find ways to keep making their products during prohibition, but also many private individuals took special delight in making their own home brews. They turned legal fruit juices into illegal wines and even learned to make passable beer. Some were just having fun, thumbing their noses at authority in a relatively harmless way, and making small supplies of beer or wine for personal use. Others saw untapped opportunity in the illegal liquor trade.

Bootleggers, Moonshiners, and Rumrunners

Before prohibition, a "bootlegger" was just someone who carried a flask of liquor inside the shaft of his boot—a common practice in many parts of the country. During prohibition, the word came to mean anyone who dealt in illegal liquor. "Moonshiner" was reserved for those who manufactured it in homemade stills; "rum-runner" described the smugglers who transported whiskey from Canada, rum from the Caribbean, and just about anything else from anywhere they could get it. These lawbreakers moved their illegal cargo by boat, by truck, and even by airplane, turning booze into big business and themselves into legends of a sort.

The Canada-to-Michigan run generated its fair share of those legends. Canada was a bootlegger's paradise; a neighboring country with no dry laws and a world-class reputation for the quality of its whiskey. The "buccaneers of booze" used their wits to bring a goodly amount of that whiskey into the United States. At first, this smuggling was a neighborly business, involving people who were otherwise law-abiding citizens.

"Apparently nobody considered himself a criminal," wrote historian Larry Engelmann. "People saw a chance to make a profit on a small investment and they took it. Within a few months a new phrase had been coined to describe the outlaw activity—'rum-running.'"[2]

When professionals entered the field, drawn by profits that could be as much as 800 percent, smuggling became bolder, more organized—and a good deal less friendly. The pros moved huge shipments involving thousands of dollars. With so much at stake, violence was never far away. Dead bodies turned up in the Detroit River with alarming frequency, and a whole new class of pirates emerged to prey on their fellow criminals.

By night these pirates ran the river, looking for plunder. They highjacked loaded boats with gleeful abandon, but their favorite targets were the moneymen headed north to buy a shipment. Since the bootlegging business operated on a strictly cash basis, a large buyer might have thousands of dollars in his possession, all of it ripe for the taking.

The most cunning pirate on the river was the Gray Ghost, who specialized in robbing buyers. No one ever knew his name; only that he was from Detroit and had an undeniable flair for drama. Like some comic book bad guy, he orchestrated an image for himself. Everything about him was gray, from his hair and his clothes to the mask that he wore to conceal his features and the sleek speedboat that could outrun anything on the river. The police never caught the Gray Ghost or even learned his name. Legend has it that he died in the streets of Detroit, gunned down by a hired killer after he victimized the wrong people with one of his daring thefts.

Rum Row
Bootlegging in International Waters

Given the enormous profits to be made in illegal booze, a Florida boat builder named William McCoy decided to enter a new profession: rum-running. He started small, buying genuine Scotch whiskey in Nassau in the Bahamas and reselling it at tremendous profit in the United States. Being a savvy businessman, Bill McCoy built a reputation for selling only top-quality liquor. Other bootleggers cut (diluted) their imported stock with homemade wood alcohol, which could cause blindness, paralysis, even death. Not Bill McCoy. People could count on his stuff, and so a new expression came into the language: "the real McCoy."

Bill McCoy didn't have to go looking for customers: they came looking for him. He only had to sail from Nassau to New York, take up position outside the three-mile limit where U.S. authorities had no jurisdiction, and stand ready to receive buyers from every speakeasy and gin joint in town. Customers charged through New York Harbor in fast speedboats, loaded their purchases, and made a mad dash for shore. Before long, smugglers made it even easier for customers to find them. A whole line of ships would take position outside the harbor, and the nation's first "Rum Row" was born.

Others soon followed. Bill McCoy himself established a small Rum Row off the coast of Boston. On the West Coast, a former policeman named Roy Olmstead ran a successful bootlegging operation based on fast boats, good liquor, and low prices. Like Bill McCoy, Olmstead was a legitimate businessman who did some rum-running on the side. In 1922, he helped organize a convention that looked more like a Chamber of Commerce meeting than a criminal conspiracy.

Rumrunners from up and down the West Coast gathered openly at a Seattle hotel to set quality standards for their product, establish price guidelines, and hammer out a code of ethics to govern their behavior. The proceeding was conducted as a formal business meeting.

THE GOOD, THE BAD, AND THE DOWNRIGHT OUTRAGEOUS

Amid all this blatant law-breaking the Prohibition Bureau, an underfunded and understaffed agency of the United States government, was charged with the task of enforcing the Volstead

Act. Unlike other government workers, prohibition agents didn't have to pass a Civil Service exam or possess any special educational or occupational background to get their jobs. Agents earned a salary of two thousand dollars a year; that was less than a New York City garbage collector earned. The job was an exercise in futility; no agency could enforce a law that thousands of Americans refused to take seriously, let alone obey. The situation was ripe for graft and corruption, and often that is exactly what occurred. These low-paying agency positions could be a license to steal for anybody who didn't mind breaking a law he was sworn to uphold.

The potential profits were enormous. Many agents lived fast and spent freely: truly crafty ones could amass a fortune. Edward Donegan is a case in point; before prohibition, he scraped out a meager living selling firewood, which he gathered along the banks of Brooklyn's Gowanus Canal. In the Prohibition Bureau he became a millionaire within four months. Donegan's specialty was selling government permits authorizing purchase of alcohol for industrial, medicinal, or sacramental purposes. With an illegally obtained permit, bootleggers could buy their liquor directly from legal warehouses and government-approved producers. Speakeasy operators all over New York gladly paid Donegan's price for this kind of access to alcohol.

Not all prohibition agents were dishonest; some did the best they could with the tools at hand. Padlocking was a favorite technique, mostly because it was easy, inexpensive, and not particularly dangerous. All it took was a court order, a padlock, and a length of sturdy chain. Eager prohibition agents padlocked everything they could find: stills for making whiskey, vats for brewing beer, and speakeasies by the hundreds.

The padlocking craze took an absurd turn when somebody put a moonshine still in the hollow of a giant California redwood tree. In a clever bit of camouflage, the bootleggers hid the entrance behind a piece of canvas, painted to look like bark. An anonymous tip alerted the Prohibition Bureau. A squad of agents raided the offending tree, destroyed the still, and dutifully padlocked the premises. A sign tacked to the canvas informed the public that the tree was closed for one year for violation of the Volstead Prohibition Act.

THE LEGEND OF IZZY AND MOE

Of all the agents good and bad, Izzy Einstein and Moe Smith were the most colorful. They operated all over the East Coast, wherever there were bootleggers to arrest and speakeasies to padlock. Izzy's trademark line, "Dere's sad news," announced more than three thousand arrests in his five-year stint as a prohibition agent. *Life* magazine placed the number of arrests at closer to four thousand, with five million bottles seized for a total street value of $15 million.[3]

While tallying up this impressive record, Izzy and Moe managed to become genuine folk heroes. Neither one looked like anybody's idea of a detective. They were short, fat, and middle-aged, but they went about their business with the exuberance of kids playing cops and robbers.

Izzy excelled at disguises and undercover identities. He might go into a speakeasy as an ice truck driver making a delivery, an accident victim hobbling on a crutch, or a weird little man carrying a pitcher of milk up to the bar. Once, he posed as a victim of frostbite by first standing out in the snow until he was blue-faced and shivering. Moe then half-carried his friend into a speakeasy and shouted for help: "Give this man a drink! He's just been bitten by a frost!"[4]

As soon as the bartender complied, the frostbite victim stopped shivering: "Dere's sad news," he said, announcing yet another arrest.

"Don't Shoot, I'm Not a Bootlegger"

Not all raid stories were so funny. Undertrained and frustrated by the hopelessness of their task, enforcement agents sometimes used strong-arm tactics and took risks that endangered innocent people. In an outbreak of grim "humor" that became a nation-wide fad, thousands displayed "Don't Shoot, I'm Not a Bootlegger" stickers in their car windows.

Meanwhile, the number of victims grew. In the streets of Washington, D.C., Senator Frank L. Greene of Vermont happened to be walking past the wrong alley at the wrong time and got caught in the crossfire between agents and bootleggers. He was shot in the head. The prosperous "Gold Coast" of Michigan's Lake St. Clair was a place of elegant homes and private docks, where wealthy people expected to relax and enjoy the fruits of their labors. Prohibition turned the area into a deadly shooting gallery. High-speed chases, desperate gun battles, and wholesale arrests became routine. So many innocent people suffered property damage, false arrest, and even serious injury, that local citizens began calling for an end to the Prohibition Bureau's patrols.

Henry B. Joy, a wealthy executive in the up-and-coming automobile industry, hired a full-time watchman to prevent unauthorized use of his dock at Lake St. Clair. When the guard couldn't stop the rumrunners or the government agents who pursued them, Joy took the line of least resistance and left his property open to both sides: "I cannot . . . protect my premises against . . . smugglers or . . . against marauding federal officers," he wrote. "Of the two I would rather be visited by the smugglers because they have done my premises no damage."[5]

Far from being cowed into obedience, many Americans rebelled against prohibition. Thousands seemed determined not only to break the law, but also to have fun doing it.

THREE

"Everybody's Doing It"

Fads and Fashions of the Jazz Age

Some called prohibition the Jazz Age. Writer F. Scott Fitzgerald coined the term in 1922, and it stuck. It was the perfect name for a time of instant heroes, when speakeasies offered watered-down booze and trumped-up glamour, professional advertising men turned selling into an art form, and America began her love affair with the automobile.

The Speakeasy Mystique

The speakeasy was a unique product of prohibition: smoky, noisy, glamorous—and illegal. Many who wanted to thumb their noses at authority in a relatively harmless way flocked to speakeasies in search of forbidden pleasures. The secrecy surrounding these establishments only added to their appeal. Many people found a thrill in sneaking down a darkened staircase, knocking on an unmarked door, and whispering a secret password to a hulking doorman.

In this glittering, illegal world, a statuesque blonde known as "Texas" Guinan held court as the undisputed Queen of the Speakeasies. Everything about her seemed larger than life; brash and brassy, she combined a mixture of city sophistication and homespun humor. Born Mary Louise Guinan on a ranch near Waco, Texas, in 1884, she had a brief and undistinguished career in silent movies before she found her niche in the fashionable speakeasies of New York and Chicago.

Her trademark greeting, *"Hello, suckers!"* welcomed the rich and famous to the shadow world of prohibition-era nightlife. Money and booze flowed freely as patrons paid $1.50 for a drink of watered-down scotch, and $25 a bottle for "champagne" that was nothing more than sparkling cider laced with alcohol. Everybody knew it wasn't champagne, but nobody cared.

In Texas Guinan's clubs, respectable middle-class people rubbed elbows with mobsters and movie stars, politicians, sports greats, and captains of industry. They could dance and watch lavish floor shows with plenty of long-legged chorus girls in skimpy costumes. With a little luck, they might even be around when prohibition agents raided the place. Where else could would-be sophisticates dance, get drunk, and flaunt an unpopular law, all at the same time? Getting raided only added to the fun.

The speakeasy seemed to hold a special fascination for women, who were experiencing new freedom for the first time in their lives. The Nineteenth Amendment (passed August 26, 1920) had given them the right to vote, but it was the Jazz Age that showed them how to throw off their inhibitions. They'd grown up believing that "nice girls" didn't drink, smoke, dance, or wear makeup or short hairdos. Now many women cheerfully bobbed (cut short) their hair, painted their faces, and raised their hemlines. In other words, they became *flappers*. Not only did they have fun, but as an added bonus they managed to scandalize the older generation in the process.

Mr. Ford's Miracle Machine

The automobile was as much a part of the mystique of the Roaring Twenties as the speakeasy and the flapper. It came into its own when the legendary Henry Ford perfected the moving assembly line. Everything from raw materials to cars under construction was placed on waist-high conveyor belts, which moved past the stationary workers at about six feet per minute. By the mid-1920s, the Ford plant could turn out a Model T in ninety minutes, and the price of the car dropped from $950 to $290. At that price, practically everybody wanted a car; by 1929 more than twenty-three million Americans owned one.

Mass production was not without its problems. The cars were absolutely standardized, and workmanship was not always of the highest caliber. Proud Model T owners seemed to find the deficiencies of their cars endearing. They even told jokes about their cars with affectionate chuckles. One favorite quip asserted that you could get a Model T in any color you wanted—so long as it was black. Another explained how to judge speed in a Model T (which had no speedometer): at 15 mph, the windshield rattled, at 20 mph, the fenders rattled, at 25 mph your teeth rattled—and at 30 mph, your fillings dropped out. Jokes aside, the Model T was a stunning success.

SHEIKS AND SHEBAS

College students were among the first to structure their social lives around the automobile; it fit in with their self-image as bold trendsetters. At a time when many people didn't go to high school, a college education was an expensive luxury, reserved for the sons and daughters of the well-to-do. In their privileged world, fashion counted for a great deal and pledging the right fraternity or sorority was a matter of the utmost importance. Satirical cartoonist John Held dubbed these adventurous young people "sheiks" and "shebas." The names stuck, and soon the students themselves used them with pride. Being a sheik or a sheba meant adopting certain mannerisms, fashions, and interests. Above all, it meant knowing how to "cut loose" and have fun:

Shieks wore sweaters, Argyle socks, and bell-bottomed flannel trousers. They slicked their hair with a dressing that made it look freshly varnished, and sported bulky raccoon coats that hung to their ankles. Shebas "bobbed" their hair, wore skirts that reached barely to their knees, and smoked cigarettes in long, ivory holders. Shieks and shebas drove around in topless Model T Fords and built their social lives around the "big [football] game" on Saturday afternoon.[1]

A Time for Heroes

Lots of hoopla surrounded college football. There were bonfire rallies and marching bands, cheerleaders, pom-pom girls, and school banners waving from the goal posts. Most of all, there were heroes. In an age of exuberance and audacity, they were more important than ever.

Sports served them up gladly; made-to-order heroes who could run, hit, catch, or throw better than anyone else. In football, there was Harold "Red" Grange, who once scored four touchdowns in twelve minutes, and Knute Rockne, the legendary Notre Dame coach who virtually invented the forward pass. In prizefighting there was a former bar brawler named Jack Dempsey, who won fifty-nine of his first sixty fights and became a millionaire in the bargain.

Of course there was the pug-nosed street kid who could hit a baseball farther and faster than anyone else. His name was George Herman Ruth, but everyone called him "Babe." In 1920, he hit fifty-four home runs. He had a lifetime batting average of .342. Babe Ruth was the perfect hero for an era of excesses. He ate too much, drank too much, and cared nothing at all for "good manners."

Babe Ruth was hardly traditional hero material, but Charles Lindbergh would have fit the same mold as Lancelot and Hercules. Tall, boyishly handsome, and well-mannered, "Lucky

Lindy" captured the imagination of the world with his historic transatlantic flight on May 20–21, 1927. Alone in the little airplane he had christened *Spirit of St. Louis*, Lindbergh flew from New York to Paris, becoming the first to complete a journey so dangerous that half a dozen men had already died trying. F. Scott Fitzgerald marveled at Lucky Lindy's achievement: "In the spring of '27 something bright and alien flashed across the sky. A young Minnesotan who seemed to have nothing to do with his generation did a heroic thing and for a moment people set down their glasses in the country clubs and speakeasies and thought of their old best dreams."[2]

READ ANY GOOD BOOKS LATELY?

Fitzgerald was something of an expert on "old best dreams"—and also on the passions of the Jazz Age. He became a central figure of one of the most vibrant periods in American literature. Other writers who figured prominently in this creative scene were Ernest Hemingway and Sinclair Lewis, the first American to win the Nobel prize for literature.

In novels such as *Main Street* and *Babbitt*, Lewis offered withering examinations of small-town life and small-town people. For some unexplainable reason, both novels became runaway bestsellers among the very people they were meant to satirize. To Jazz Age intellectuals "Gopher Prairie, Minnesota," might have been the hometown from hell, and George Babbitt a shallow and mediocre "average man." But to millions of Americans Gopher Prairie sounded a lot like home, and Babbitt wasn't so bad once you got to know him.

Both Fitzgerald and Hemingway largely ignored the conforming majority to write about the disaffected and disillusioned rebels of the twenties. Hemingway made his name with *The Sun Also Rises*, a spare, understated look at the wanderings of Lady Brett Ashley and her entourage of rootless companions. Fitzgerald was already a best-selling author when he wrote *The Great Gatsby*, about the rise and fall of a shady financier, whose career of excess and failure seemed to parallel that of the Jazz Age itself. Though *Gatsby* is widely recognized as Fitzgerald's finest work, it was not a strong seller when it came out in 1925.

In the literature of the 1920s, none of the characters seem to know quite what they were supposed to be doing, or why they were supposed to be doing it. The self-satisfied Babbitts stumble through life without doubts or passions or torturous uncertainties. The Gatsbys and the Lady Brett Ashleys dash headlong to destruction for no particular reason other than perhaps boredom and a nagging purposelessness.

"It's All the Rage"

While writers created best-sellers and the Charles Lindberghs of the world made history, ordinary folk had to be content with lesser exploits. Young people wanted to test themselves against new obstacles, and if obstacles happened to be in short supply they cheerfully manufactured a few. A steady progression of fads and crazes flashed on the American scene, only to vanish when the next fad came along. Strange games and ludicrous competitions were all the rage. People competed to see who could swallow the most live goldfish; talk, whistle, or sing the longest; or shove the most sticks of chewing gum into their mouths.

Flagpole sitting had to be one of the oddest endurance tests ever devised. It started in 1924, when an ex-boxer calling himself "Shipwreck Kelly" first did it as a publicity stunt for a Hollywood theater. The idea caught on, and soon "daredevils" all over the country were perched on the top of flagpoles, trying to set a new record. Shipwreck Kelly logged a total of 145 days on top of flagpoles during a 1929 tour of the country.

Dance marathons were another fad that began in the 1920s. Entrants didn't have to be good dancers; this was no contest of skill but an endurance test, with thousands of dollars in prizes going to the couple who could stay the course. The rules were simple: keep dancing until you drop. The last couple on their feet won the competition. It was not an activity for the faint of heart. One young woman read that bare-fisted prizefighters pickled their hands to toughen them before their fights, and decided to give the method a try. Mary Promitis soaked her feet in brine and vinegar for nearly a month, preparing for a 1928 dance marathon. Promitis didn't win—but not from lack of trying. She was still on her feet when officials shut down the dance as a health hazard. The contestants had been at it for three full weeks.[3]

Most people chose less strenuous forms of recreation. Americans by the millions became crossword puzzle addicts, experimented with Ouija boards, and devoted endless hours to an ancient Chinese game called *Mah-Jongg*. Played with 144 tiles, *Mah-Jongg* then was complex and confusing; the perfect game for a decade of uncertainty and profound change. The rules seemed to mirror life; hazy to begin with and subject to constant change. Nobody could ever pin them down once and for all, because different rule books gave different—and often wildly conflicting—interpretations. The only way to play was by agreeing ahead of time on which set of rules a particular game would follow. That amounted to making up the rules as you went along.

In the Roaring Twenties, people faced a bewildering array of decisions about how to spend their time and money. They became a generation of potential customers just when American business was learning how to use advertising to create a need for products that nobody ever needed before. The result was America's mass market economy.

"SELLING THE SIZZLE"

The mass market economy got a boost from a new class of professional "admen" who taught American business the fine art of "selling the sizzle instead of the steak." In other words, they glamorized everything from toothpaste to convertibles, promoting images over actualities. Advertisers went for glitz and glamour, promising success, happiness, and romance to anyone who bought the "right" product.

Radio had a special relationship to commercial advertising; in a sense, they "grew up" together. America's first commercial radio station, KDKA in Pittsburgh, was licensed in 1920. A year later, factory-produced radios appeared on the market, replacing the homemade crystal sets early radio fans had used. By 1924, radio broadcasting was a multimillion-dollar industry, reaching an audience of twenty million people. Sound became a sales tool: some companies saw a bright future for the new medium and became sponsors of regular programs: *The Eveready Hour,* a musical-variety program sponsored by Eveready Batteries, came on the air in December 1923; *The Collier Hour,* debuted in 1927, offered variety segments and serialized dramas; and *The Chase and Sanborn Hour,* sponsored by the coffee company of the same name, began as a music program in 1928.[4]

Advertising was breaking new ground, and it did not always do so in the best of taste: "marking the ads of the '20s were several traits that they shared with the decade itself, such as brashness and a lack of scruples," said *Time.* "Many ads trafficked in quasi-factual, pseudoscientific details: a mouthwash boasted the approval of exactly 45,512 doctors, none of them named, and a shaving cream stated . . . that it expanded 250 times with water."[5]

Most advertising made a fairly direct statement about the benefits of the product: Woodbury's Facial Soap gave the user "A skin you love to touch." Coca-Cola offered "The pause that refreshes" and Maxwell House Coffee was "Good to the Last Drop." The delightfully zany "Quick, Henry, the Flit!" ads illustrated the benefits of Flit insect repellent at a glance, with the slogan and a cartoon showing a character under attack by a large—and obviously determined—mosquito.

It was with the automobile that advertising stepped over the boundary that divides substance from image. This "psychological style" of advertising bypassed practical uses altogether to connect the product to the consumer's innermost fears and desires. It started with the Jordan Playboy, a flashy roadster that was created by an advertising copywriter rather than an automotive engineer. Ned Jordan designed the car to look bold, innovative—and expensive. Then he wrote an ad to sell it. Today, hardly anyone remembers Ned Jordan's car, but his ad, "Somewhere West of Laramie" is a classic example of how to sell the sizzle instead of the steak.

The advertisement contains not a single word about the car's design or engineering features—no nuts-and-bolts descriptions of its transmission or valve system or brakes. There's just a prose poem about a "broncobusting, steer-roping girl" somewhere west of Laramie who "loves the cross of the wild and the tame." The car itself is a thing of "laughter and lilt and light" and to own it is to be at one with "the spirit of the lass who rides, lean and rangy, into the red horizon of a Wyoming twilight."[6]

Selling the sizzle became easier with the beginning of charge accounts. Until the 1920s, Americans were accustomed to paying cash for all their purchases. A home mortgage was acceptable, but any other form of debt was regarded as unwise; even shameful. The automobile changed that perception. It was in a category by itself; as the prices dropped, more people could afford a car, but not as a one-time cash purchase. Consumer credit was born, and before long the question was no longer "do we have the money?" but "can we get the loan?" The standard of living soared, especially among the middle class, and Americans demanded more possessions, more experiences; more of absolutely everything.

To many Americans, the lure of "buying now and paying later" became irresistible. They went on a spending spree, going deeper and deeper into debt as they accumulated possessions they could never afford before. Few of these people stopped to think that they were buying things today with "money" they hoped to earn tomorrow.

FOUR

THAT'S ENTERTAINMENT!
Broadway, Harlem, and Hollywood

Until the 1920s, there was no "entertainment industry" as such. Large cities had concert halls, opera houses and theaters; small towns made do with occasional visits by touring theatrical companies, circuses, and vaudeville (musical-variety) troupes. Feature-length silent movies were added to the mix as early as 1908; but Hollywood, that legendary "movie capital of the world," came of age in the twenties. Like the wildly popular radio shows that were broadcast into American living rooms, motion pictures blended technology with entertainment, added a dash of fantasy, and swept the country. The result was what we have come to call "mass culture."

Arts and entertainment became saleable commodities like automobiles and argyle socks. In New York City it was a time when Broadway was not so much a street as a state of mind, and Harlem was the place to be on a Saturday night. In Chicago, African-American musicians from New Orleans filled the speakeasies with jazz, while in California a quirky band of visionaries built the motion picture industry out of celluloid film and leftover dreams. Prohibition added a devil-may-care recklessness to this creative growth.

"The Lullaby of Broadway"

According to historian Herbert Ashbury, Broadway was once an elegant avenue of restaurants, theaters, and palatial hotels. Profits for many of these establishments depended on the sale of fine wines and spirits (distilled beverages such as whiskey and gin). Prohibition put dozens of them out of business, and transformed Broadway into "a raucous jungle of chop-suey restaurants, hot-dog and hamburger shops, garish nightclubs, radio stores equipped with blaring loudspeakers, cheap haberdasheries, fruit-juice stands, dime museums, candy stores and drugstores, speakeasies, gaudy movie houses, flea circuses, penny arcades, and lunch counters that advertised EATS!"[1]

This brazen new Broadway may have been less refined than before, but it still offered access to serious theater for those who were interested. Audiences turned out to see the dramas of Eugene O'Neill as well as just-for-fun musicals like *Padlocks of 1927*, a prohibition satire that starred none other than Texas Guinan in her one and only Broadway role.

Broadway's most famous contribution to the popular culture of the Roaring Twenties actually began in Harlem, with a show called *Runnin' Wild*. This joyous musical review was a product of the "Harlem Renaissance," a movement that brought African-American music, art, and literature to a general audience.

Runnin' Wild featured a dance that was a wild explosion of knocking knees, flying beads, and snapping fingers. It required the discipline of a trained dancer to learn and the endurance of a marathon runner to perform—hardly the kind of thing that should have caught on with the general public: but it did catch on. Within a year it swept the country. Within a decade it was immortalized as the timeless symbol of an era. They called the dance the Charleston, because it was loosely based on a folk dance that originated in Charleston, South Carolina.

Music and dance came from the very heart of Harlem. African Americans sang the blues and loved it, beat out jazz rhythms and loved that also. They danced with wild abandon and joined in the generalized rebellion of the decade's flaming youth. This was, after all, the Jazz Age, and young African-American performers were on its cutting edge.

In their exuberance, these performers made Harlem the focus of a glittering nightlife: "Harlem," wrote David Levering Lewis in his introduction to *The Portable Harlem Renaissance Reader*, "filled up with successful bootleggers and racketeers, political and religious charlatans . . . street-corner pundits and health practitioners . . . and hard-pressed, hard-working families determined to make decent lives for their children. Memories of the nightspots . . . of Bill 'Bojangles' Robinson demonstrating his footwork on Lenox Avenue, of raucous shows at the Lafayette [theater] . . . have been vividly set down by [writers of the period]."[2]

At the height of the renaissance, Harlem attracted large crowds of elegantly dressed white people, who packed the famous Cotton Club to dance to Duke Ellington's band, then drifted into the smaller cabarets to hear such performers as Gladys Bentley and Bessie Smith sing the blues. Some African Americans welcomed these white visitors; others were less than enthusiastic, as poet and novelist Langston Hughes explained:

> *White people. . . . packed the expensive Cotton Club on Lenox Avenue. But I was never there, because the Cotton Club was . . . for gangsters and monied whites. They were not cordial to Negro patronage, unless you were a celebrity like Bojangles. So Harlem Negroes did not like the Cotton Club and never appreciated its Jim Crow policy in the very heart of their dark community. Nor*

did ordinary Negroes like the growing influx of whites toward Harlem after sundown, flooding the little cabarets and bars where formerly only colored people laughed and sang, and where now the strangers were given the best ringside tables to sit and stare at the Negro customers—like amusing animals in a zoo.[3]

Red-Hot Jazz and Low-Down Blues

Some whites no doubt came to Harlem because it was the fashionable thing to do, but others came for the music; for the blues. It wailed, it pounded, it throbbed like nothing they had heard before. It captured the soul of the times. Blues singers were a breed apart; almost all were women with big, soulful voices who didn't so much sing the music as *become* the music, letting heartbreak and pain sound through every note. The lyrics were simple, repetitive, and phrased in the language of the street. There was nothing high-toned about authentic blues.

In the rhythm of the blues, any self-respecting fan can practically hear the deep-voiced wail of Bessie Smith, "empress of the blues." During the early twenties when the blues was in vogue, she made more than 150 recordings and performed to legions of adoring fans. When audiences began to lose interest in the blues toward the end of the decade, Bessie adapted to the change in public taste by adding some mainstream popular numbers to her repertoire.

While the blues mourned life's pain and hardship, jazz attacked them full tilt, trumpets blaring. Jazz began in turn-of-the-century New Orleans and traveled up the Mississippi with the majestic riverboats, which transported cotton, gamblers, and jazz bands from river town to river town. By 1920, New Orleans jazz arrived in Chicago in the person of Joseph "King" Oliver and his Creole Jazz Band.

"There was an audience waiting for them," wrote Geoffrey Perrett, "the tens of thousands of southern blacks who longed to hear their own music again and were able to pay for it. . . . Gangsters also liked jazz. It was the music of outcasts, after all. But it also filled their speakeasies and nightclubs with a strident, brassy sound, creating an atmosphere of excitement that kept the customers coming."[4]

That "atmosphere of excitement" was a major ingredient in mass culture. Flaming youth of the Roaring Twenties wanted larger-than-life amusements, full of crash and thunder and flashes of light. Like jazz and blues, movies were made to order for that kind of flamboyance. Everything about them was glamorous, endlessly compelling to a generation that enjoyed fantasizing about itself.

Prohibition With Palm Trees

By the time the Eighteenth Amendment took effect in 1920, Charlie Chaplin and Mary Pickford were everybody's favorite movie stars, with million-dollar salaries to match their fame. A sleepy little town called Hollywood had become the "movie capital of the world," complete with gated studios, elaborate restaurants and movie theaters, and streets lined with palm trees imported from Hawaii.

Director D. W. Griffith was the prime mover of early Hollywood; a man with the vision to experiment with the possibilities of film. In his hands, movies became more than just stage plays on film. Griffith developed camera techniques such as flashbacks, fade-outs, and close-ups, which would become staples of the filmmaker's art.

Unfortunately, he first used these new techniques in a controversial film called *The Birth of a Nation* (1915), which glorified the racist Ku Klux Klan of the post–Civil War South. The film provoked widespread protest and was blamed for several lynchings. To redeem himself, Griffith then produced *Intolerance* (1916), depicting the evils of intolerance in four parallel stories. By the strong public reaction they provoked, both films hinted at the enormous impact the motion picture industry would have on the popular culture of the Roaring Twenties.

Many of the people of Los Angeles were neither all that impressed by the cultural potential of movies nor all that fond of the wild-living strangers in their midst. Los Angeles was heavily populated with elderly midwesterners, who had come to California to retire in the sunshine and brought their heartland values with them. Writer Louis Adamic coined the term "Folks" to describe these seniors, and he was less than complimentary when describing their way of life:

> No matter where one goes and what one does, one cannot get away from The Folks in Los Angeles. They are everywhere and their influence is felt in well-nigh every phase of city life. They are simple, credulous souls; their bodies are afflicted with all sorts of aches and pains, real and imaginary; they are unimaginative and their cultural horizons are sadly limited—and as such they are perfect soil to sprout and nourish all kinds of medical, religious and cultural quackery.[5]

The Folks took prohibition seriously, and so did the Los Angeles police. By the midtwenties, the Central City Jail was processing fifty thousand bookings a year, the majority for prohibition-related offenses.[6] When the police crossed paths with movie people, the results could be anything from disastrous to hilarious as one investigative reporter discovered:

> At 2:30 a.m. one hears in the upper reaches of the Jail House a sudden outburst of screams and oaths. . . . Going down to the [finger]print room to observe, one finds that a bevy of movie queens have been pinched on charges of drunk-driving . . . resisting an

officer, etc., and are in a fair way to being fingerprinted. . . . Gin,
temperament . . . general cussedness and a certain knowledge that
they will soon be out again all combine to make for a general melee
and an interesting close-up. In the group are a star of worldwide
fame, the sister of another famous celebrity, near stars, maids in
waiting, and a bevy of attending sheiks and bull fighters, everybody
more-or-less cock-eyed drunk. . . .[7]

"READY WHEN YOU ARE, C.B."

Movie director C. B. De Mille was the heir apparent to the pio-
neering D. W. Griffith. De Mille was a master of innuendo with
the ability to walk the thin line that divided the merely
"naughty" from the outright indecent. C.B., as he was known,
possessed an unerring sense of popular taste. When he saw that
moviegoers wanted glamour and a whisper of scandal, he gave
them lush productions with gorgeous leading ladies, dashing
leading men, and suggestive titles like *The Golden Bed* and *Forbidden Fruit.*

When outraged moral reformers tried to have his movies
banned, De Mille blunted their criticism by producing a film
with epic scope, lavish sets and costumes, and surefire subject
matter. *The Ten Commandments* (1923) became the first of De
Mille's trademark biblical epics and helped make him the most
influential director of the Roaring Twenties.

De Mille's movies not only reflected public taste, but also
helped shape it. He hired the finest makeup experts, hairstylists,
and fashion designers, and put them to work creating an on-
screen world where beautiful people led lives of high adventure,
untroubled by ordinary concerns. In matters of fashion, the
wealthy looked to the elegant salons of Paris for inspiration; the
middle class looked to the movies.

On the set, De Mille was an absolute dictator who blew a silver bugle to signal his huge casts of extras into action. Nobody questioned C. B. De Mille, or second-guessed him. When he gave an order, he didn't want to hear arguments or excuses. He just wanted to hear one thing: "Ready when you are, C.B."

In the end, none of the excesses of Hollywood or Harlem could match those of the criminal subculture that developed during prohibition. As general lawlessness blurred the line between right and wrong, good and evil, a whole new breed of criminal appeared: the professional gangster, who made crime and violence a way of life.

FIVE

CRIME GETS ORGANIZED

Making Crime Into a Business

The Mob, the Mafia, the Outfit, the Organization: by any name, organized crime was the most sinister development of the Roaring Twenties. This wasn't freelance rumrunners trying to make a dishonest dollar while they had the chance; this was crime as a business like any other, complete with executives, midlevel managers, and production workers—otherwise known as "bosses" "enforcers" and "soldiers."

Prohibition fit perfectly into the plans of these career criminals. The law was unpopular, widely ignored, and easily broken. To many people, it didn't seem like a "real" law at all, so they were not inclined to get overly upset with those who made a living from breaking it.

In his biography of crime boss Al Capone, Laurence Bergreen explained:

> Before Capone and the Prohibition era, the public and law enforcement agents clung to notions of criminals—their motives, their personalities—dating back to the previous century. Criminals, it was believed, chose to be evil; indeed, they relished their wickedness, their depravity, and cruelty. And they were loners, outcasts.

In the 1920s, however, criminals such as Capone entered the main-
stream of society, acquiring vast economic power. They espoused
[middle class] values, built homes, took care of their families, tried
to teach their children the difference between right and wrong. . . .
Their organizations mimicked the customs and structure of conven-
tional businesses. They practiced a rudimentary form of charity.
They could deliver social services to people with no access to the le-
gitimate political system.[1]

BUILDING AN UNDERWORLD

Structured criminal organizations existed to one degree or another in most major cities of prohibition America, yet only one
city had the dubious honor of becoming the Crime Capital of the
World: "Chicago . . . ignored prohibition from the start," wrote
Jack Kelly in an article in *American Heritage* magazine. "Many saloons simply kept operating. More secretive speakeasies joined
them, as did blind pigs—grocery or hardware stores that fronted
for grogshops [liquor stores]. The importation of juniper oil, used
to flavor homemade 'gin,' skyrocketed. For those with political
connections and a propensity toward lawbreaking, a career as a
bootlegger offered almost limitless wealth."[2]

The "city of the Big Shoulders," as poet Carl Sandburg
dubbed Chicago, was a raw-boned prairie town where the smell
of stockyards and slaughterhouses was inescapably *there*, meaning
everywhere, and politics was a down-and-dirty game that nobody
seemed to win. Crime gangs existed in Chicago long before prohibition. At the turn of the century, the infamous Levee district
was the site of a vast criminal substructure, with youth gangs
looking for trouble, pickpockets looking for victims, and so many
brothels that the madams who ran them actually had their own
"professional organization," the Friendly Friends.

In 1912, a new mayor declared war on Chicago vice and shut down most of the Levee brothels. Vice, however, didn't disappear; it simply moved, spreading to the surrounding neighborhoods like a virulent infection. By 1914, "Big Jim" Colosimo was the acknowledged vice lord of the city, running a far-flung criminal empire while keeping his job as a street sweeper for the city.

By 1919, with prohibition still waiting in the wings, an independent Chicago Crime Commission had already noted a disturbing new trend in the underworld: "Modern crime, like modern business, is tending toward centralization, organization, and commercialization. Ours is a business nation. Our criminals apply business methods."[3]

JOHNNY TORRIO, THE THINKING PERSON'S RACKETEER

The man who put the "organized" into organized crime was as unlikely a mobster as anyone could imagine. Johnny Torrio was a small man, slightly built, with the face of a contentious bank clerk who always balanced his books to the penny. Torrio saw no reason that crime shouldn't pay—and pay plenty—without gang warfare or other costly unpleasantness.

Torrio became Big Jim Colosimo's business manager in 1909 and promptly began to structure the operation for greater efficiency and profitability. When Big Jim fell before an assassin's bullet on May 11, 1920, Johnny Torrio took over the criminal empire he had helped create. From a strictly business standpoint, the timing of this rise to power could not have been better: prohibition was in its infancy, with unlimited potential for profit to the organization that could exploit it effectively—and Johnny Torrio stood in a position to do just that.

His first act as boss of Colosimo's crime empire was to pay

homage to the fallen leader at a funeral so lavish it set the tone for all the gangster funerals to come. Priests and police captains were among those who turned out to pay their last respects to Chicago's most notorious vice lord. Amid a dazzling display of pomp and circumstance, a procession of five thousand mourners followed the hearse to Oakwood Cemetery. Honorary pall bearers included three judges, an assistant state attorney, and nine city councilmen. There were wreaths and bouquets enough to gladden the heart of any florist as the city of Chicago said goodbye to Big Jim Colosimo. In an unaccustomed display of public emotion, Johnny Torrio wept before the assembled members of the press, mourning the loss of a man he had loved like a brother. By the next day, though, the underworld rumor mill was circulating a story that Torrio had paid $10,000 to have Colosimo "taken out of the picture."

Torrio soon built the "business" into a multimillion dollar enterprise that was too big for any one man to run alone. Bowing to the inevitable, he sent to New York for a young man who had been his protege in the "rackets" (organized crime)—a personable, twenty-two-year-old named Al Capone.

Capone was the exact opposite of Torrio; flashy, hungry for publicity and approval, interested as much in "being somebody" as in running a business. Under Torrio's tutelage, Capone restrained his natural inclinations, and the two of them set about making Chicago a safe and civilized haven for crime.

By 1924, the major gangs of Chicago had their respective territories, the minor gangs knew their place, and an uneasy peace reigned in the underworld. The Torrio-Capone mob controlled most of the south side, an irrepressible Irishman named Dion O'Banion controlled the north side of town, and a family of six Sicilian brothers known as the "Terrible Gennas" had turned bootlegging into a cottage industry in the centrally located neighborhood called Little Italy.

THE ALKY-COOKERS

The Gennas ran what was arguably the most inventive bootlegging operation in Chicago. They obtained a government authorization to produce industrial alcohol and paid dozens of impoverished families in Little Italy the sum of $15 a week to tend small copper stills in their homes.

Each week, the brothers made the rounds of producers' homes, picking up the supply of homegrown "hooch" (alcoholic beverage) and transporting it to a huge warehouse just four blocks from a police station.

The product was "dreadful stuff. . . . It stank, it was raw, and it was dangerous. Brewed quickly, on the cheap, the Gennas' whiskey teemed with toxins. Real whiskey acquired its distinctive golden hue from the wooden casks in which it is slowly and patiently aged. But the Gennas had no time for the careful distillation of whiskey; instead, they colored it with caramel, or coal tar, and flavored it with fusel oil, a noxious by-product of fermentation normally removed from whiskey lest it cause severe mental disturbance or even insanity."[4]

Quality was not a big consideration with the Gennas' customers. The brothers made millions, peddling their poison. It sold so well that they gradually expanded the business into Dion O'Banion's northside territory. O'Banion went to Johnny Torrio for help. As the acknowledged peacemaker of the underworld, Torrio tried to arbitrate the dispute. He didn't get very far; the Gennas were in no mood to negotiate. They smelled money and they had no intention of being thrown off the trail by Dion O'Banion.

THE FLOWER MAN

The reckless, devil-may-care O'Banion had an improbable front for his illegal activities: he owned half interest in Schofield's

Florist Shop, where he spent many pleasant hours arranging blooms for a variety of occasions. His specialty was funerals: lavish gangland funerals, to be exact. It turned out to be a nice little sideline. Mobsters thought nothing of spending several thousand dollars on flowers to honor a fallen rival—even when they were the ones who'd killed him.

Profitable as gangster funerals could be, selling flowers would never bring the kind of money O'Banion wanted. For that, he needed the rackets—and for the rackets, he needed a territory that no other gangster, including the Terrible Gennas, would dare to violate. When Torrio's peacemaking efforts were less than successful, O'Banion took it on himself to hijack a truckload of the Gennas' poisonous home brew.

Johnny Torrio now had his hands full, convincing the Gennas not to retaliate with an all-out attack. O'Banion further complicated matters by cheating Torrio and betraying him to the police. Pleading distress over his tense situation with the Gennas, the clever O'Banion announced his intention to retire from the rackets. He was tired, he said. He planned to move to Colorado and live quietly somewhere in the Rocky Mountains.

As soon as he could settle his affairs in Chicago, he would be on his way. But there was the matter of the Sieben Brewery to be settled. O'Banion owned the brewery in partnership with Torrio and Capone. Would they be interested in buying his share? Torrio gladly paid $25,000 for O'Banion's one-third of the business, and counted himself lucky to be getting rid of the troublesome Irishman without bloodshed.

The sale was really a masterful swindle. From his contacts at police headquarters, O'Banion had learned that the police planned to raid the brewery on the night of May 19, 1924. Not only did he sell Torrio a brewery that would soon be out of business, he also contrived to have his former partner on the scene when the police came crashing through the door. O'Banion, who had no previous police record, got off with just a warning. Johnny Torrio, who had a prior conviction, was sentenced to nine months in jail.

The florist actually bragged about how he had bested the hotshot leader of Chicago's underworld. That chortling was his final mistake; peacemaker or not, Johnny Torrio had his pride. He wasn't going to take that kind of treatment from anyone. Dion O'Banion's days were numbered. On November 10, 1924, the florist died in his own shop, cut down by Mike Genna and two hired gunmen who frequently worked for the Torrio-Capone organization. In the best gangland tradition, the treacherous O'Banion received a grand funeral, with eulogies by prominent figures and a cortege of ten thousand people to escort him to his grave. The flowers were beautiful!

A Shattered Peace

As soon as O'Banion was laid to rest, his chief lieutenant Hymie Weiss (real name: Earl Wajciechowsky) set out to take revenge on Torrio, Capone, and the Gennas. Weiss was something of a legend in criminal circles; he invented the assassination ploy that would be immortalized in dozens of gangster movies— forcing the victim into a car and "taking him for a ride" to his own assassination.

Weiss and his henchmen never got the opportunity to take Johnny Torrio for a ride, but they did catch him offguard during a shopping trip to Chicago's famous Loop. While Torrio's wife watched in horror from their car, Weiss and a vicious upstart named George "Bugs" Moran stood over her fallen husband, firing bullets into his body. No one, least of all Johnny Torrio's doctors, expected the businessman-gangster to survive, but somehow he did.

Three of the six Genna brothers fell victim to the gangster

wars that followed the O'Banion slaying. The surviving Gennas went into hiding, fearing for their lives. Their bootleg operation, which had provided work and a weekly wage for dozens of immigrants, simply faded from the scene.

Johnny Torrio was never the same after his brush with violent death. His body was weakened, and his spirit was crushed by the failure of his plan for a "civilized" approach that would make racketeering a business like any other. He decided to retire, turning the operation over to his faithful friend and lieutenant, Al Capone.

Bossman Al Capone

Once in control of the Torrio empire, Capone courted the spotlight as avidly as his mentor had avoided it. His style was brash and brazen, but he could also be charming at times. He once paid thousands of dollars to save the eyesight of a passerby who was injured in the crossfire of a gangland assassination. He loved handing out Christmas presents to the children in his sister's school, and was unfailingly generous to those he counted as friends—and sometimes, even to his enemies.

When a crusading newspaper reporter wrote an exposé on one of his brothels, Capone sent four thugs to beat up the man, then turned around and paid his hospital bill. When the reporter recovered and went back to work, he discovered that Capone had bought the paper, leaving him no choice but to work for the notorious gangster or quit his job. The reporter quit.

Not all of Capone's enemies were so easily neutralized. Since the O'Banion killing, Hymie Weiss and "Bugs" Moran had not stopped trying to get Capone. The undisputed king of Chicago racketeers took to traveling in a specially built armored limousine, surrounded by bodyguards carrying tommy guns and wearing the pearl grey fedoras that became a Capone organization trademark.

When repeated efforts to make peace with Weiss had failed, Capone ordered him killed. A pair of out-of-town assassins, expert machine gunners, came to Chicago to do the job. On October 11, 1926, they gunned down Hymie Weiss in front of Schofield's Florist Shop, where his late boss Dion O'Banion once held court as the flower man of the Chicago underworld.

My Deadly Valentine

Bugs Moran took over the O'Banion-Weiss gang. Moran was widely regarded as "crazy," prone to violent tempers and casual murders. As Weiss's lieutenant, he had been a thorn in Capone's side; as Weiss's successor, he was a threat that could not be tolerated. Capone decided it was time to eliminate Moran and the remnants of the O'Banion-Weiss gang in a single, master stroke of violence. On February 14, 1929, at ten o'clock in the morning, four gunmen posing as police shot down seven of Moran's men against the back wall of the S.M.C. Cartage Company warehouse. Moran himself wasn't in the warehouse that day.

For the first time in his sordid career, Al Capone had gone too far. The Valentine's Day Massacre aroused a public outcry all over the nation and drew the unwelcome attention of the federal government. From that time forward, Al Capone was a marked man. Eliot Ness, the federal agent made famous in the television show *The Untouchables*, tapped Capone's telephones and dogged his steps, and a meticulous U.S. attorney named George E. Q. Johnson built the case that would send Chicago's top mobster to Alcatraz for tax evasion: in October 1931, Alphonse Capone was sentenced to eleven years in federal prison.

SIX

A Piece of the Action
Schemes and Scandals in Public Life

Sharp operators were as much a part of the Roaring Twenties as racketeers, rumrunners, and movie stars. Scandals rocked the White House, predatory real estate developers and stock speculators became overnight millionaires, and many ordinary people charged headlong into the fray, intent on grabbing their own piece of the action. At the same time, America struggled to come to terms with changes so far-reaching that they had shaken the very foundations of the national identity.

Warren Harding's Washington

The presidency of Warren G. Harding was riddled with corruption. Though Harding himself seemed to be an honest man, he had a troublesome knack for surrounding himself with dishonest ones. He was a senator from Ohio in 1920, when the Republican party made him its candidate for president. He was chosen largely because he didn't hold any strong opinions that would compromise him as a candidate. He won the election for the same reason. Unfortunately, the lack of focus that made him a good candidate made him a weak and ineffectual president.

Harding came into office with no real viewpoint, no agenda of things he wanted to accomplish. If he had a goal, it was popularity: " 'I can't hope to be the best President this country's ever had,' he admitted one night. 'But if I can, I'd like to be the best-loved.' "[1]

As president, Warren G. Harding was more like an actor playing a role than the leader of a great nation. He knew how to appear dignified without being stuffy, authoritative without being dictatorial—in other words, how to appear "presidential." The rest was all smoke and mirrors.

A political rival once characterized Harding's speeches as "an army of pompous phrases moving over the landscape in search of an idea."[2] Harding coined his own term to describe this flowery, overwrought style of oratory that had been popular during the nineteenth century: "bloviating" he called it, presumably from the same slang roots as *blowhard*.

Bloviating was hopelessly outdated, but it still worked among the small-town rural folk who were Harding's natural constituency: it was less effective in the august chambers of the U. S. Congress: "[W]hat could thrill a crowd of farmers at a picnic or state fair tended to fall flat on the Senate floor. [Harding's] oratory was immovably set in the nineteenth-century style, with an emphasis on outflung arms, an abundance of patriotic clichés, and the fervent . . . 'Oh, Senators!' "[3]

THE "OHIO GANG"

It is not surprising that a man who felt so out of his element would surround himself with longtime cronies and friends. The "Ohio gang," as they came to be called because so many came from Harding's home state, became his personal refuge from the turbulence of national politics. The president enjoyed nothing so much as playing poker and drinking with his buddies. They gathered at the White House two or three evenings a week for a high-stakes game.

Alice Roosevelt Longworth, daughter of Theodore Roosevelt, happened to be visiting at the White House while one of these games was in progress. She saw "the study . . . filled with cronies . . . the air heavy with tobacco smoke, trays with bottles containing every imaginable brand of whiskey stood about, cards and poker chips ready at hand—a general atmosphere of waist-coat unbuttoned, feet on the desk, and the spittoon alongside."[4]

The boys-will-be-boys poker games could have been just an endearing foible of a popular and well-loved president if Harding hadn't also appointed several of his cronies to important positions in his cabinet. That was a decision he lived to regret. His most disastrous selections were Charles R. Forbes as head of the newly formed Veterans Bureau, Harry M. Daugherty as attorney general, and Albert B. Fall as secretary of the Department of the Interior.

Forbes was a wisecracking, genial charmer who knew how to manipulate people as instinctively as a cat knows how to toy with a mouse. He parlayed his new job into a private gold mine, arranging large "commissions" for himself with the company that built several new veterans' hospitals, and taking kickbacks from suppliers who provided such homey necessities as floor wax and cleaning materials at highly inflated prices. When Forbes finally got caught with his hand in the till, his assistant and accomplice, Charles F. Cramer, committed suicide rather than face the consequences of his actions.

"THE LITTLE GREEN HOUSE"

Harry Daugherty, a lawyer by profession, was not smooth enough for "high society," or principled enough for weighty responsibility. He looked like what he was: a minor-league politician. But through the fortunes of politics and the friendship of Warren G. Harding, he ended up as attorney general of the United States.

When Daugherty came to Washington, he brought his friend Jessie Smith along. Smith was flabby, pleasure-loving, and exceedingly good-natured. He took life as he found it, and if he found it full of goodies, so much the better. While Daugherty worked at the Department of Justice, Smith spent much of his time at a place on K Street that was to become known as "the little green house."

According to Geoffrey Perrett, the house was "a combination card parlor, speakeasy, house of assignation [secret or illicit meetings], and bribery exchange. . . . Jess Smith could be seen on the corner greeting . . . visitors . . . and humming a line from that hit of the early twenties, 'My God, how the money rolls in!' "[5]

BROKEN PROMISES, BROKEN LIVES

When Harding began hearing rumors about the unsavory doings in the little green house, he ordered Harry Daugherty to send Smith back to Ohio. The attorney general of the United States could ill-afford to be connected to someone involved in such disreputable doings, the president said. Daugherty had no choice but to comply, though the banishment obviously crushed Jessie Smith. Stripped of the heady sense of being in the thick of things, he became increasingly morose. After a time in exile, Jessie Smith returned to Washington. There, on May 30, 1923, he committed suicide by firing a single bullet into his brain. The scandal Harding tried so hard to avoid could no longer be kept secret, and the president was deeply shaken.

Harding decided to take a cross-country tour, relaxing from the stresses of office by doing what he did best—whistle-stopping through the country, "bloviating" to the small-town crowds who showered him with unqualified affection and admiration. Harding never returned from that trip. He died in San Francisco on August 2, 1923, from a cerebral hemorrhage or a coronary thrombosis. That same night, Vice President Calvin Coolidge was sworn in as president.

As Harding's funeral train made its way to Washington along

hastily cleared tracks, crowds gathered in every town and hamlet, standing in silent mourning for a president whose greatest desire was to be loved. The people of America honored him as one of their own; a common man, and decent, unmoved by the hunger for power that afflicted most politicians. At that time, Warren G. Harding had his wish.

A Place Called Teapot Dome

Fortunately, Harding didn't live long enough to see that love turn to outrage and disgust. For even as the nation mourned, the Senate was investigating yet another scandal connected with the Harding administration. This one involved questionable leases on land that had been set aside as government oil reserves—and the trail led straight to Secretary of the Interior Albert Fall. Fall was a former senator from New Mexico, known for a certain flamboyance of style but generally respected as an able administrator. When news of his appointment as secretary of the Department of the Interior reached the Senate floor, Fall was confirmed by a standing ovation from his colleagues. There were no questions, no doubts, and most important, no confirmation hearings or background investigations.

Fall's first official act was to look into the matter of government oil reserves. Three prime oil fields were set aside for future use by the navy; two in California, and one in Wyoming at a place called Teapot Dome. It was a shame, Fall thought, that these rich deposits would go untapped. In 1921, he decided to do something about it.

Over howls of protests from conservationists who wanted to forestall development as long as possible, Fall leased the Teapot Dome reserve to Harry F. Sinclair's Continental Trading Company. A similar arrangement turned one of the California reserves over to Fall's old friend and business partner, Edward L. Doheny.

Investigations revealed that Fall had received a $100,000

"loan" from Doheny, and $300,000 in cash and negotiable securities from Harry L. Sinclair. Eventually, both leases were canceled by the federal courts, and Albert Fall became the first Cabinet officer in U.S. history to go to jail for bribe-taking and conspiracy.

The repercussions of the Teapot Dome scandal tarnished Harding's reputation beyond repair. People simply could not believe that all this maneuvering had happened without Harding's knowledge. The late president was obviously guilty of *something*; at the very least, negligence and incredible gullibility. The public turned against this man they once loved.

THE FIRST OF THE GREAT CON MEN

Whatever Warren G. Harding did or did not do while he was president, it is difficult to believe that he started out with anything but the best of intentions. That was not the case with Charles Ponzi, the man who ran the first big swindle of the Roaring Twenties.

Ponzi got the idea for his scam while he was a $20-a-week clerk in the office of J. P. Poole, a Boston-based trader in foreign currency. The company, Ponzi decided, was too cautious and too ethical; there was a fortune waiting to be made in the currency market for someone with big ideas and a small conscience.

With $100 that he had saved from his modest salary, Ponzi opened the Old Colony Foreign Exchange Company. He only needed a few "investors" to get his scheme off the ground; he found them by offering a 50 percent profit in just ninety days. To the financially unsophisticated—or the merely greedy—the plan made sense. Ponzi simply proposed to buy international money orders in countries whose currency was down on the world market and resell those money orders a few weeks later in countries whose currency was up. A handful of people decided to give the scheme a try; exactly ninety days later, they received $15 for every $10 they had invested.

Charles Ponzi was hailed as a miracle worker, financial genius, and all-around good guy. People stood in line to give him their money, and the "foreign exchange trader" continued to pay as promised. At the height of its success, Ponzi's Old Colony Foreign Exchange Company was taking in a million dollars a week. Ponzi never really invested the money at all. In what became known as a pyramid scheme, he simply used the funds from new "investors" to pay off older ones. So long as there were enough new investors coming in, Ponzi was able to keep up the front. The bubble burst on August 16, 1920, when Old Colony went out of business and Charles Ponzi went to jail for fraud.

In the get-rich-quick boom days of the twenties, there were plenty of other unethical operators waiting to take his place. In New York, the soaring stock market was at the mercy of speculators and manipulators who cared nothing at all for the long-term consequences of their short-term strategies. Even decent, law-abiding citizens wanted to get in on the boom. The location of the New York Stock Exchange, "Wall Street" became synonymous with the stock market, in the same way that "Broadway" meant theater and "Madison Avenue," advertising.

In 1927, Harvard University economist William Z. Ripley told President Calvin Coolidge about the "prestidigitation, double-shuffling, honey-guggling, hornswoggling and skulduggery"[6] happening on Wall Street. Unfortunately, neither man knew what the federal government could—or should—do about it, so their response was to do nothing at all. The stock market became a powder keg, just waiting to explode.

"OCEANFRONT PROPERTY"

Real estate developer Carl G. Fisher was not himself a scam artist; he was a visionary who unknowingly paved the way for the biggest land grab of the twentieth century. It all began when Fisher visited Florida; a place of jungles and swampland that also happened to have the most idyllic climate he had ever experienced. Fisher and his investment partners drained the swamps, cleared the jungle, and created the Florida real estate boom.

Others were quick to seize the opportunities that presented themselves. Hard-sell real estate agents took potential buyers on free bus tours, complete with complimentary lunches and lengthy harangues about the glories of Florida real estate. Ten percent down reserved a lot. Prices went up so quickly that some people didn't bother buying lots at all—they just reserved them with 10 percent down, then sold the reservations (called "binders") at a handsome profit. Hundreds of people bought Florida land sight unseen, dealing through the mail with fly-by-night companies that promised a chunk of paradise and as often as not delivered worthless swampland.

In 1926, when Florida Fever was already showing signs of peaking, a massive hurricane slammed into the coast. By the time the storm ended, the death toll stood at four hundred, and property damage was estimated at $300 million. Stunned residents surveyed the devastation and realized that even paradise had its downside. The value of Florida real estate plummeted. Oceanfront property that had sold for $2,000 a foot dropped to $700. A rash of bankruptcies and foreclosures cleared out the speculators and hard-sell promoters, bringing the greatest land boom of the decade to a shameful end. The speculators turned their attention from Florida real estate to other, more promising, opportunities.

PLAYING THE MARKET

In 1928 and early 1929, America went on a stock buying spree. Banks, brokerage houses, and big-money speculators started the action, and many smaller investors soon followed. Suddenly everybody seemed to be talking about the fortunes to be made on Wall Street.

The growth was truly phenomenal: the number of shares traded jumped from 317 million at the end of 1919 to more than one billion at the end of 1929. Stock values skyrocketed; for example, in March 1928, Radio Corporation of America stock went from $90 to $109 per share in a single week. A person who bought fifty shares at the beginning of that fateful week could realize a profit of $900 in just seven days: no small amount at a time when the average worker earned $750 a year.[7]

At the same time, there were some signs of economic weakness and instability: bank failures here and there, bonds that even the promoters viewed as risky, and banks and brokerage houses heavily committed in "margin accounts."

Buying on margin was a favorite trick of speculators because it enabled them to control more stock than they could actually afford to buy. The investor put up only a small percentage of the money for a purchase, borrowing the rest from the brokerage or bank. When the stock went up, the investor could sell all his shares at a profit, repay the broker with interest, and still make a tidy bundle on the deal. By September 1929, American investors owed $8.5 *billion* for their margin purchases; more than twice the entire federal budget of $3.1 billion for the year.[8]

Many ordinary people who had never played the stock market decided to give it try, largely because of the efforts of men like Charles E. Mitchell. Mitchell, the adventurous young president of the National City Bank of New York, was an incurable optimist with bold ideas, who wanted to shake up the stodgy world of high finance. It was his idea to market stocks and bonds the way one might sell automobiles and refrigerators; he planned to get "the little guy" involved in what had been a rich man's game.

Mitchell hired crack salesmen who were accustomed to using high-pressure tactics, then spurred them on with contests, with $25,000 in prizes for the top producers during a given period. The strategy brought thousands of small investors into the market and some of them did very well: "On one of his trips to New

York in the late '20s, F. Scott Fitzgerald found that his favorite barber had retired, having made five hundred thousand dollars in the stock market. Trust executors and small-town bankers shifted funds out of business loans and government bonds into stocks. The moguls of Wall Street assured them that the stocks could only go up."[9]

The moguls were wrong. On Tuesday, October 29, 1929, the bottom fell out of the stock market and the American economy plunged toward disaster. Banks failed, businesses closed, millionaires became paupers, and middle-class people who had tried to invest with the big boys got crushed in the landslide. Many people didn't realize it yet, and some resolutely closed their eyes to the truth, but the days of skimming and scamming and playing the stock market like it was a roulette wheel were coming to a close. Soon it would be time to pay the piper.

SEVEN

WORKING STIFFS
Organized Labor in Transition

For working-class Americans, the decade that roared was never some grand and glorious party—it was a struggle for survival. Without strong unions to fight for them or government regulations to protect them, working people were trapped in a cycle of poverty that few could hope to escape.

THE WORK ETHIC

To be "working class" in 1920 meant something very different from what it means today. The typical industrial worker was unskilled and would accept whatever wages and working conditions the employer happened to offer. By 1929, factory workers made only five cents more per hour than they had in 1921, and nearly half of American families had an income of less than $1,500 a year.[1]

Child labor was an unfortunate but accepted part of working-class life. The 1920 census identified 1.1 million "gainfully employed" ten- to fifteen-year-olds, not counting those tens of thousands who worked as temporary labor in the fields during the peak agricultural seasons of planting and harvest. The census also failed to count children under ten who worked afternoons and weekends for as little as 20¢ an hour. They did jobs such as attaching buttons to cards and finishing artificial flowers, sitting at long tables in cold, cheerless rooms.

The "work ethic" that helped build this country turned work into a moral issue. "Good" people were hard workers, "bad" people were lazy, and truly superior people knew how to work for the sheer joy of working: in the words of Theodore Roosevelt, "It is only through labor and painful effort . . . that we may move on to better things."[2]

As long as American society could believe in the nobility of work, it was easier to ignore the haggard children carding buttons, and the factory workers who put in twelve-hour days on grim and noisy assembly lines. There was no such thing as sick leave, overtime pay, medical insurance, or retirement plans. There was just work; endless, grinding work for as long as you could stand it.

Attempts to form labor unions met with strong resistance. Since the Russian Revolution of 1917, the specter of communism had made any sort of collective action immediately suspect to most Americans. With all their talk about solidarity and the struggle of "the masses," labor unions sounded dangerous—even to many of the very working people they were trying to help.

Employers took advantage of this vague feeling of unease to force workers to sign "yellow dog" contracts, in which they promised not to join or form unions. Many an attempted strike was abandoned because of a court injunction that made the strikers into lawbreakers. The unions, which had been gaining ground in the years before World War I, fell victim to the mood of the country. Even the American Federation of Labor (AFL), one of the most conservative labor groups in the country, saw its membership drop from five million in 1920 to less than three million by 1929.[3]

Important developments in society don't conform to the calendar; every decade is influenced by people, events, and ideas from earlier ones, and the 1920s was no exception. Two strikes that began in the autumn of 1919 had a profound effect on the decade that roared.

Men of Steel

Of all the jobs in heavy industry, few were more demanding than steel production. The work was not only hard, but also dangerous. In the 1920s, hundreds of mill workers were injured or killed, yet the companies had no safety training programs and no protective equipment or attire. Health and safety measures boiled down to a single Slavic word: *tchekai*—"watch out!" In the 1922 book *Steel: The Diary of a Furnace Worker*, Charles Rumford Walker recalled the impact of that single, shouted word: "It's a word that is ringing in your ears all night. Watch out for the crane that is taking a load of hot metal over your head . . . watch out for the load of hot cinder coming down . . . for the trainload of hot ingots that passes your shoulder."[4]

Given hazardous conditions, low pay, and long hours, it is not surprising that disaffected steelworkers launched the first industrywide strike of the twentieth century. It started when William Zebulon Foster, a labor organizer with a reputation for radical ideas and risky policies, decided to attempt what no one else had been able to do: organize the steel mills.

He knew it wouldn't be easy. The steel companies owned the towns where workers lived, and they kept a tight hold on their property. They had a network of informers, and a private police force called the "coal and iron police," which was paid by the steel industry and sanctioned by the local government. When strike talk was brewing, the coal and iron police broke up every large meeting they could find. They needed no warrant, no evidence, no proof; the smallest suspicion was reason enough for them to act.

Being inventive as well as dedicated, William Foster knew how to organize in secret. The companies didn't pay much attention when little social clubs with harmless-sounding names started popping up in mill towns. Despite such efforts, organizing was sporadic at best. The majority of the steelworkers were immigrants who spoke little English and did not have a history of union activity. Most labor leaders thought the situation was hopeless, but Foster kept plugging away.

On September 22, 1919, his work paid off: more than 350,000 steelworkers in ten states walked off the job. Fifty steel towns came to a grinding halt, leaving the entire industry in disarray. The strike held until November, when one of the AFL-affiliated unions, the Amalgamated Association of Steel, Iron and Tin Workers, voted to break the strike and return to work.

Although the defection involved only a small percentage of the total number of strikers, it was a death blow, nonetheless. The Amalgamated members were the skilled elite of the steel mills, highly trained for specialized jobs. When they abandoned the strike and returned to work, the companies brought in outsiders for the unskilled jobs. In those early days of labor organizing, strike-breaking did not have the stigma it would carry fifteen years later. Most of the replacement workers knew nothing of labor activism; they had never belonged to a union. They only knew that they could get jobs in the steel mills, so they came.

There was nothing William Foster and his mill hands could do to stop the flood of new workers. By December, the remaining strikers and their families were huddled in grim tent cities, trying to last out the winter against hunger, sickness, and impossible odds. In January 1920, they gave up. While the rest of the country celebrated a new decade and stockpiled alcoholic beverages against the onset of prohibition, the steelworkers struggled to put their lives back together.

Though the great steel strike of 1919 was a failure, it nonetheless became a landmark in labor history, revealing a problem that would plague union organizers for years to come: unskilled workers had no bargaining power. They could be replaced and the companies knew it. Not until the National Labor Relations Act of 1935 would the law fully protect workers' right to strike and to establish unions.

An Unlikely Victory

The coal miners fared better than the steelworkers. In 1919, a young labor organizer named John L. Lewis stepped into the fray. This burly, barrel-chested young man had quit school at the age of twelve and gone to work in the mines. He had joined the United Mine Workers (UMW) in 1906. For many children of the mining towns, that would have been the end of the story: quit school, go into the mines, work there until you die. John L. Lewis wanted more.

He educated himself with the help of a sympathetic young schoolteacher who later became his wife. In a debating society, he revealed a gift for oratory that was to hold him in good stead throughout his adult life. He could thunder with the best of them; eyes flashing, fists pounding the lectern, powerful voice reaching out to grab an audience and hold them spellbound. He could also develop a carefully reasoned, logical argument. In 1919, he got a chance to put those skills to the test.

During World War I, the coal mining industry had operated under a "no strike" agreement between the UMW and the government called the Lever Act. Coal was still the nation's principal fuel, and to stop producing it in the middle of wartime need—for any reason—seemed unpatriotic, even treasonous. The miners were willing to do their part to help America in the Great War, so they waited and did not complain.

With the end of the war came the end of the no-strike agreement, or so the miners thought. When the companies refused to give pay increases that were already overdue, the UMW called a strike to begin on November 1, 1919. The government countered with a court injunction. War or no war, the Lever Act was still in force, they said. The miners could not strike.

Lewis and his intrepid miners defied the order. Unlike the steelworkers, who were already breaking ranks, the UMW held firm. On December 19, just twelve days before the start of the new decade, the coal miners won a 31 percent raise. A wage of $7.50 a day made them the highest paid workers in American industry. In recognition of his accomplishment, John L. Lewis was elected president of the United Mine Workers, a post he was to hold for the next forty years.

WORKING FOR MR. PULLMAN

Another labor leader who began his career in the 1920s was A. Philip Randolph, founder of the first African-American labor union in history, the Brotherhood of Sleeping Car Porters (BSCP). At first, Randolph seemed entirely unsuitable to the task he had chosen. He'd never seen the inside of a Pullman sleeping car, let alone worked on one. He was the college-educated son of an itinerant preacher, well dressed and well mannered, with a cultivated "Harvard accent" that set him apart from the people he meant to help.

Randolph chose to organize the porters because they were also set apart; the elite among African-American workers, in their immaculate white jackets and shiny black shoes. The first porters hired by George Pullman to tend his elegant railroad sleeping cars were former slaves, eager to make their way in a free society. Pullman found them perfect for the job. They were accustomed to waiting on people, able to take orders, and willing to work for near-starvation wages.

What started as a practical hiring decision soon grew into a tradition. By the twenties, all but a handful of Pullman porters were African Americans. Being a Pullman porter was a source of pride for the men themselves and for their families. Unfortunately, as A. Philip Randolph pointed out, pride didn't put food on the dinner table. Porters worked under difficult conditions for low wages. Out of a base salary of less than $70 a month, they had to buy their own meals, pay for lodgings at stopovers, and purchase a minimum of two uniforms a year.

They were also required to give many hours of unpaid time to the company. When a porter was assigned to a car, he was expected to see that it was spotlessly clean, stocked with linens and all other supplies, and ready to receive passengers. When the passengers arrived, it was his duty to get them settled in their compartments, put away their luggage, and perform any other services that might be needed. A porter didn't earn a cent until the train pulled out of the station and the shift officially began.

Standby duty was also an unpaid requirement of the job. On standby, a porter had to present himself at the station, dressed and ready for work. He might wait for several hours without ever being assigned to a car—or being paid a cent. The company always called more standbys than it expected to need, so many men were eventually sent home with no car—and no wages.

This wasn't right, A. Philip Randolph told the porters, and in time they began to listen. On August 25, 1925, the BSCP held its first organizational meeting and declared itself a valid union. Exactly what that meant from a practical standpoint, not even Randolph could say. In the antilabor atmosphere of the day, the best he could hope to do was keep the union together and be ready to seize the moment when it came.

The moment never did come in the twenties. It took a stock market crash, the repeal of prohibition, and a whole new set of labor laws before the union was in a position to mount its first strike. On August 25, 1937, exactly twelve years to the day from its first organizational meeting, the Brotherhood of Sleeping Car Porters became the first African-American labor union to be recognized by a major American company. When A. Philip Randolph signed the labor contract, he not only fulfilled his own dream, he secured $2 million worth of pay increases and benefits for the long-suffering Pullman porters.

The Tragedy of Sacco and Vanzetti

On April 15, 1920, a daring payroll robbery at a shoe factory in Braintree, Massachusetts, left two men dead and led to one of the most controversial criminal trials of the century. Eyewitnesses to the crime saw two of the assailants, both of whom "looked Italian."[5]

On May 5, Nicola Sacco, a shoe worker, and Bartolomeo Vanzetti, a fish peddler, were arrested for the crime. They were working-class Italian immigrants who spoke little English; known anarchists (opponents of all forms of government) who carried guns, and draft dodgers who once fled to Mexico to avoid having to register as required by law.

Their trial before Judge Webster Thayer was a travesty of justice. Thayer was a self-important little man with a hard mouth and a rigid mind. Having decided that Sacco and Vanzetti were guilty, he apparently had no intentions of letting a little thing like the law get in the way of their conviction. On the bench, he behaved more like a prosecutor than a judge, and off the bench he referred to the defendants as "those anarchist bastards."[6] On July 14, 1921, Sacco and Vanzetti were found guilty of murder in the first degree.

There was a major outcry from socialists, radicals, and prominent intellectuals all over the world. No less an authority than Professor Felix Frankfurter of the Harvard Law School (later to become a chief justice of the Supreme Court) wrote an article arguing that the two men were innocent and setting forth the many ways in which their trial had been a mockery of the American legal system. Repeated motions for new trials kept the men alive on death row, but in late summer of 1927 the appeals and legal maneuvering ran out. Sacco and Vanzetti died in the electric chair on August 23, 1927.

Outside the prison and in the streets of cities all over the world, sympathizers marched and mourned. Bartolomeo Vanzetti's eloquent summation of all that had happened and what it had meant doubtlessly echoed in many people's minds:

> *If it had not been for these thing, I might have live out my life talking at street corners to scorning men. I might have die, unmarked, unknown, a failure. Now we are not a failure. This is our career and our triumph. Never in our full life could we hope to do such work for tolerance, for justice, for man's understanding of man, as now we do by an accident.*[7]

Justice denied is a common theme that often runs through the treatment of immigrants and unskilled workers during times of social upheaval. These people on the lowest rung of the social ladder got caught in the crossfire between the wild and wicked excesses of the Roaring Twenties and the sometimes rigid conventionalism of small-town America. It was not a comfortable place to stand.

EIGHT

JUST PLAIN FOLKS

Rural Society Defends "The American Way"

The louder the twenties roared in speakeasies, gangster hide-aways, and at scandalous Hollywood parties, the harder rural Americans hung onto the familiar values that anchored their world. In countless small cities and country towns, the twenties hardly roared at all, unless it was in fury at the licentiousness of the Jazz Age.

"THE AMERICAN WAY"

The decade saw a major population shift in the United States, from a rural society of farms and small country towns to an urban one of bright lights, crowded streets, and big business. Life changed so fast that some people couldn't keep up with it.

While the cities tried to be "modern" and sophisticated in all things, small-town America reaffirmed family and community. Never mind Albert Einstein's "fool theories" about the workings of the universe, not to mention Charles Darwin's ideas about evolution. Never mind speakeasies and gangsters and young women with bobbed hair. Everything a decent person needed to know was "in the book"—the Bible.

Morality was an absolute in small-town America; right was right and wrong was wrong. Good people were honest, thrifty, trustworthy, industrious, and "neighborly" to a fault. Bad ones were the opposite. The men joined lodges with secret oaths and funny hats; the women belonged to the sewing circle and the garden club; the children to the Scouts.

Everyone worked hard, and while there was a great premium on sociability, the pursuit of pleasure for its own sake was somehow decadent and unworthy. Except for small boys on occasional summer afternoons, having fun was suspect; not sinful, perhaps, but certainly frivolous and bordering on the irresponsible.

LIVING IN THE CRACKS

Critics who scorned this way of life often missed one important point: for millions of people, it worked just fine. The problem was not with those who stayed in their safe little world while the larger society moved past like a fantastic circus parade and vanished without trace. The problem was with those who fell between the cracks; uncomfortable with the old way, unable to fit in with the new.

Some people got pushed into the cracks by widespread economic changes over which they had no control. Beginning in 1920, American agriculture was staggered by a number of problems. The American Relief Administration discontinued its policy of buying surplus wheat to send to needy populations all over the world. Wheat prices plummeted as a result. Prohibition devastated the markets for barley and grapes, while the growing popularity of paper bags reduced the need for cotton. With markets so curtailed, many small farmers lost their land, and those who were able to hang on had to make every nickel work like a dime.

Some farmers blamed the government for their predicament, some blamed "foreign influences," and some feared that it was punishment from God for the rampant immorality of Jazz Age society. It was not a good time to be asking questions or experimenting with new ways of life. Many adults held tightly to the old and familiar while just as many young people dabbled in the new and exciting. The result was the country's first real generation gap.

Even in conservative towns where tradition was respected, youth wanted to have its fling. Teenagers who still went to church on Sunday mornings saw nothing wrong with going to movies and dances on Saturday night. They wanted to buy automobiles someday and to live in houses with electric lights and telephones.

In a culture that still regarded eight grades of school as the norm for decent, respectable folk, some kids not only wanted to go to high school, but also to college. The very thought of sheiks and shebas with their wild parties and freewheeling ways chilled God-fearing parents to the core.

They'd heard stories, awful ones, about how college life abounded in immorality, and if it didn't turn kids into loafers and "bums," it would turn them into rebels who mocked what their parents held dear.

The Palmer Girls[1]

Even when young people didn't get within a hundred miles of a college or a big city, it was difficult to keep them isolated from the onrush of new ideas. The three daughters of Charles and Molly Palmer are a case in point. (The Palmer family is real and so are their stories. But to protect the family's privacy, some of the names in this account have been changed.) They lived in a small town in North Carolina; the girls grew up during the Roaring Twenties, reared with values their parents considered to be absolute and unchanging.

Lucy, the eldest, had beautiful long legs, which she wasn't allowed to show, and a noticeable overbite, which she couldn't manage to hide. Dottie was a typical middle daughter; sweet-natured and rather passive, with a lazy streak that bothered her parents immensely. Libby, the baby of the family, had naturally wavy hair, huge brown eyes, and an unfortunate tendency to plumpness. She also had what people called "a mind like a steel trap," so her mother dutifully taught her to hide it. Smart women scared men away, said Molly Palmer, quoting the wisdom of her contemporaries. Smart girls would end up bitter old maids unless they learned to behave themselves.

Being an old maid was the second-worst fate for a girl: the first was to become a "fallen woman." Molly was immensely proud of her own virtue. She'd never so much as been with her husband unchaperoned until the day they were married. After twenty years and three children, she could honestly claim that Charles, her husband, had never seen her unclothed.

It was Molly's dearest wish that her daughters be as virtuous as she had been; that they all have white weddings to men who would treat them kindly and support them well. That was the way of things, after all. Right and wrong were always and everywhere the same; of that Molly was sure, and all the bobbed hair and skimpy clothing in the world couldn't change her mind.

In the sanctuary of the Palmers' two-story frame house, the Jazz Age didn't exist, and Flaming Youth was an ugly rumor. Then Charles bought a Model T Ford, and Lucy taught herself to drive the thing. A fast-talking shoe salesman from Conley's Department Store started calling on Dottie, and Libby kept her nose in a book.

Molly began delivering little lectures to her daughters about how a young woman could find "her prince." She talked about the importance of staying pure for the wedding day, and told the girls with utmost sincerity that unkissed lips were the most queenly gift they could bring to the altar. She didn't understand why Dottie giggled.

For the sake of her daughters Molly tried, but the lure of the Jazz Age was just too strong. When the crash of 1929 ruined the family business, Lucy packed her things into the old Model T and went to the city. She found a job cashiering, moved to a drab boardinghouse, and turned herself into an old maid with an overbite, a cashier's squint, and beautiful long legs nobody ever got to see.

Sweet little Dottie ran off with the shoe salesman, who turned out to be an alcoholic. He drank himself to an early death, leaving Dottie with three daughters and an uncertain future.

Libby stopped reading all the time, but then she ate to make up for it. Next thing anybody knew, she weighed 250 pounds and married a mean-spirited man who expected her to wait on him hand and foot and wasn't above knocking her across the room if she didn't move fast enough to suit him.

Until the day Molly Palmer died, she blamed the "loose morals" of the Roaring Twenties for bringing her family to grief. Like most people who believe that standards of behavior are fixed forever, she couldn't change with the times.

People like Molly often respond to new situations by clinging all the harder to old ways. Sometimes, this distrust of the new and different can bring out the worst in people. In the Jazz Age, it triggered a revival of the Ku Klux Klan.

RETURN OF THE NIGHT RIDERS

The Klan of the 1920s was different from the post–Civil War vigilante groups that terrorized and murdered former slaves in the South. The revived Klan wasn't just after African Americans; this time, it targeted everybody who wasn't a white Protestant Christian and set itself up as the guardian of truth, decency, and public morals.

It all began on Thanksgiving night in 1915 at Stone Mountain, Georgia. A former circuit-riding Methodist preacher named William J. Simmons led a small group of followers up the mountain. They made a large wooden cross, wrapped it in straw and oil-soaked rags, and raised it in a prominent place. Impatiently they waited for nightfall, and when it came they set the cross aflame. That burning scar against the night sky signaled the birth of "the Invisible Empire, Knights of the Ku Klux Klan."

Simmons chose that name for its historic significance and to capitalize on the recent publicity surrounding D. W. Griffith's controversial pro-Klan film *The Birth of a Nation*. He threw in elaborate rituals, hooded robes, and grandiose titles like "Imperial Wizard" and "Grand Dragon" for the leaders. A whole new vocabulary of magic and mystery awaited the initiate, all based around the letter K: Klalender (calendar), Klonklave (meeting), Klavern (local chapter), and Kloran (ritual guide).

Added to this were fiery crosses, moralistic rhetoric, and the chance to terrorize Jews, Catholics, African Americans, Italians, Russians, Asians, Mexicans, and anybody else who spoke a different language or worshipped in a different way from the Klan members. Klansmen who were more interested in morality than in race or national origin would seek out and punish homosexuals, "loose women," gamblers, drug users, and seducers of "innocent young girls."

To Simmons's great disappointment, recruiting members to the Ku Klux Klan was a slow process. Not even the strident patriotism and xenophobia (fear or hatred of strangers) of World War I brought initiates flocking to the sign of the fiery cross. By 1920, the KKK had only two thousand members and Simmons was on the verge of giving up the fight. Then he met two hotshot promoters named Edward Young Clarke and Elizabeth Tyler, and things began to turn around.

A MARKETING PLAN FOR HATE

Clarke and Tyler owned and operated the Southern Publicity Association, a firm that specialized in fund-raising and promotion. As agents for the Salvation Army and the Anti-Saloon

League, they had raised those organizations to positions of prominence. Now they stood ready to do the same thing for the Klan—for a fee, of course; a hefty percentage of the $10 initiation fee they proposed to charge each candidate.

Their plan was simple and effective; tap into the current popularity of lodges and service clubs. Small-town America was a nation of joiners, with Masons, Oddfellows, Woodmen of the World, and other such groups flourishing as never before. These groups offered varying degrees of ritual and secrecy, plus friendship, status, and the comfort of belonging to a group that functioned as protection against an increasingly perplexing and changeable society.

Clarke and Tyler proposed to do the same thing with the Klan. Borrowing Simmons's trick of making the petty sound important, they hired more than one thousand membership salesmen to work on commission and called them "kleagles." The $10 initiation fees became "klectokens."

The kleagles were instructed to play on whatever prejudices dominated in a particular locality; given the numerous groups that the Klan hated, finding suitable targets was no problem at all. They opposed Mexicans in Texas, Japanese in California, Jews in New York, and Catholics and African Americans in the Deep South.

The strategy worked. At the height of its influence, in 1924, the Klan boasted three million members, many of whom were respectable businessmen, professionals, and midlevel white-collar employees of larger companies. Because the Klan was so secretive, sources differ on its true strength; estimates run from three to four and a half million members in 1924. The Klan made inroads into government, getting its people elected to important city, county, and even state offices. Members belonged to all Protestant denominations, and apparently saw no contradiction or conflict of interest in professing Christianity while belonging to an avowedly racist hate group.

Klavern meetings typically opened and closed with prayer and the singing of the hymn "The Old Rugged Cross," which the Klansmen regarded as their unofficial anthem. Social occasions such as picnics, barbecues, and boat trips brought out members and their families for "fun and fellowship." The image at these gatherings was outwardly wholesome, and in the words of an old cliche, "as American as apple pie."

Burning Crosses, Raising Cain

The other, darker side of Klan activity had nothing whatsoever to do with picnics, politics, or apple pie. Especially in the early days of Klan power (before 1923), hooded night riders terrorized dozens of communities. They made regular forays to seek out and punish minorities and lawbreakers. Offenders were tarred and feathered, flogged, castrated, branded, or lynched. In Oklahoma, the Klan had "whipping squads" of trained floggers, who attacked prostitutes, bootleggers, gamblers, and even people who violated the "Blue Laws" (laws that forbade doing business on Sunday, for religious reasons).

To many observers, the truly frightening thing about the Klan was not that it existed, or even that it committed so many horrible acts; the truly frightening thing was that it became almost respectable. Hard-pressed police departments, swamped with prohibition-related offenses over and above the usual run of crime, looked the other way when the night riders went out to harass and punish anyone whose behavior threatened the Klan's idea of morality.

A 1923 editorial in *Christian Evangelist,* the journal of the Disciples of Christ Church in Indiana, reflected the feelings of many who were willing to overlook the terrorism because the Klan was doing something that mainstream white Protestant Christians were unable to do:

There are those who affirm that [the Klan] in its protests against lawlessness, against Roman Catholic domination, against Jewish monopolies here and there, against a divided allegiance to our country, is doing a great and needed work; that it is the savior of Protestantism; that it is the defender of the Constitution; that it is a help to morals and religion; that its masks are but legitimate appeals to the dramatic within all of us . . . that it has 'cleaned up' villages, towns and cities. . . . There can be no doubt that . . . tens of thousands of good people feel just this way about it and are fervent in its advocacy. [2]

The Klan eventually went too far. Weakened from within by power struggles in the leadership and from without by growing public concern over its tactics, its membership and influence began a downward slide. In 1925, David C. Stephenson, Grand Dragon of Indiana's powerful Klan, raped and brutalized a young woman who had tried to repulse his advances.

When the devastated victim committed suicide, Stephenson stood trial for kidnapping, rape, and second-degree murder. In an effort to save himself from life imprisonment, he informed on various Klan collaborators, including Indiana governor Edward Jackson. The scandals destroyed the Klan in Indiana and severely damaged it everywhere else. By 1930, the Klan had fewer than ten thousand members. It was finished as a force in American life, leaving a legacy of bitterness and broken promises. Disenchanted members had to look elsewhere to fill the gaping void in their lives.

NINE

"LORD, SEND A REVIVAL"
Fundamentalist Religion During the Roaring Twenties

In the confusion of their world, full of new choices, many Americans turned to the safe, secure, "old-time religion" that had comforted their parents and grandparents. Evangelists like Billy Sunday and Aimee Semple McPherson drew huge crowds to their tent meetings. Local churches became havens for desperate people in a time of spiritual confusion.

Out of that confusion grew the World's Christian Fundamentals Association, an organization formed to defend the faith against the evils of Darwinism. The Association condemned Charles Darwin as an instrument of the devil and his theory of evolution as "an attack on the Bible, a challenge to the revealed truth in the Book of Genesis, a denial of man's divine creation."[1]

BACK TO BASICS

Fundamentalism was not so much a separate philosophy as a habit of mind; a way of looking at the world from a fixed framework that had been in place for countless generations. After World War I, which had been hailed as "the war to end war," there was a great national crisis of belief. Anyone could see that

World War I hadn't ended war any more than prohibition had ended drunkenness.

In the immigrant neighborhoods of large cities, strangers worshipped their own ideas of God in their own languages; no fire from heaven struck them down. In the speakeasies and dance halls and movie palaces, supposedly respectable people engaged in sinful behavior; no prophet of the Lord appeared to condemn them to everlasting damnation. America's crisis of faith deepened, and many people turned away from religion.

Fundamentalism was the counterattack to this rampant unbelief; in its own way, it was as important to the Roaring Twenties as prohibition. Both appealed to traditional values at a time when tradition was falling by the wayside. Prohibition was supposed to protect body, mind, and morals; Fundamentalism concerned itself with the soul.

The concept was straightforward, simple, and uncompromising. There was no room for argument on the main points, though various groups of Fundamentalists debated such topics as the proper method of baptism ("sprinkling" vs. total immersion) and whether one ought to kneel or stand to pray. Morality, like doctrine, was set once and for all in the Holy Bible and could not be adapted to changing social conditions.

Billy Sunday Gets the Call

William Ashley Sunday was born in Ames, Iowa, on November 19, 1862. He was a rangy, good-looking kid with the fluid grace of a natural athlete. Before he began his preaching career, he played professional baseball for the Chicago White Stockings.

Billy Sunday made his mark as an evangelist during the temperance crusade of the 1910s, preaching religion and prohibition as the pillars of "righteousness." His most famous sermon, preached dozens of times all over the country, wasn't a call for sinners to come back to God, but for drinkers to come back to abstinence (refusal to drink alcoholic beverages). This pulpit-pounding ex-baseball player cast a long shadow:

"It is impossible to quantify his influence in prohibition legislation," noted Sunday's biographer Lyle W. Dorsett, "but most observers agreed that he helped make nineteen states dry. . . . He also campaigned hard for national prohibition."[2] A popular song of the twenties heralded Chicago as "the town that Billy Sunday could not shut down," alluding to the colorful preacher's reputation for "shutting down sin" wherever he spoke.

To Billy Sunday, sin was death and death was awful; he had feared it since childhood, when everything around him turned into death. He was five weeks old when his father died. Before he reached his sixth birthday, he had lost his stepfather and three-year-old half sister, four aunts, an uncle, and the grandmother he adored.

It was his grandmother's death that devastated the little boy's world. On the second day after her funeral, young Billy disappeared from his home. After a frantic search, the family found him on top of his grandmother's grave, sobbing and shivering, lying in the November snow. He almost died from exposure. Billy Sunday never did learn to accept death and loss. He learned how to *pretend* to accept what no human being could prevent, but inside he needed something more. It was this need to defy death that transformed an engaging young baseball player into the most famous evangelist of his day.

Preaching was a big step. Sunday had almost no formal education; his language was a grammarian's nightmare, his imagery homespun and completely lacking in theological sophistication. ("Going to church don't make anybody a Christian any more than taking a wheelbarrow into a garage makes it an automobile."[3]) On the podium, he whooped and yelled and bounced around, endlessly haranguing "sinners" about the danger of damnation and the terrible depths of their sin.

Something about the young preacher reached people: he was

physically attractive, obviously sincere, and he had a sixth sense about how to reach the hard-pressed farmers and townspeople of middle America. He gave them a Jesus they could understand; brave, determined, able to face the worst life had to offer—and able to help them do the same: "Jesus was no dough-faced lick-spittle proposition," he told his rapt listeners. "Jesus was the greatest scrapper that ever lived."[4]

During Billy Sunday's years of greatest prominence (1910–1920) huge crowds greeted him everywhere he preached and donated "love offerings" that ran into the hundreds of thousands of dollars. In a single New York City rally, Sunday collected $120,500. He and his wife, Nell, began to enjoy their success a bit more than a wary public considered proper. The Sundays traveled in elegant Pullman cars, wore fine clothes, owned a nine-room home in Indiana and a ranch in Oregon. They spent money as they pleased, accounting to no one for any of it.

Eventually there was a scandal and bad publicity that cost Billy Sunday his standing as America's premiere evangelist. In a twist of irony, the man who fought so hard for traditional values and did so much to advance the cause of prohibition, gradually went out of favor in the decade he helped create.

After 1921, he was no longer invited to preach in major cities. The size of the towns he visited fell steadily downward, as did the size of the audiences and love offerings. By the time Billy Sunday died (November 6, 1935), Fundamentalists were inclined to overlook his excesses and credit him for his undeniable contributions to their movement.

JOY COMES IN THE MORNING

Aimee Semple McPherson was even flashier than Billy Sunday, with a preaching style that made the old pulpit-pounder look tame. Born Aimee Elizabeth Kennedy on October 9, 1890, in Ontario, Canada, "Sister Aimee," as everyone came to call her, was the daughter of a Canadian farmer and a Salvation Army worker many years his junior.

She started her preaching career by traveling around the country in an open Oldsmobile she called the "Gospel car." When she held her first independent revival meeting in August 1915, she was just twenty-five years old, already twice married, once widowed, and the mother of two young children.

Sister Aimee was an immediate success on the revival circuit. If Billy Sunday had made religion quite literally a matter of life and death, then she made it *fun*. Instead of beating people over the head with their sin and terrorizing them with threats of everlasting damnation, Sister Aimee emphasized the joy and fulfillment of the Christian life.

Aimee Semple McPherson belonged to the twenties—and the twenties belonged to her. It is difficult to imagine Sister Aimee in any other decade. She had the passion, the flair, the audacity of the decade that roared. She also had a knack for fitting what she believed to be a timeless message into inventive, contemporary forms.

After her days on the road, Sister Aimee settled in Los Angeles during the heyday of silent movies. In February 1921, she broke ground for the lavish, five-thousand-seat Angelus Temple; there she worked amid the glitz and glamour of Hollywood, perfectly at home as the contemporary of movie stars, sports heroes, slick operators, and, of course, "The Folks"—those midwestern seniors who formed the bulk of her congregations. Sister Aimee gave them all a show. She didn't just preach sermons—she staged them, complete with music and lights and costumes and dialogue. It was pure religious theater and the people loved it.

SISTER AND THE NIGHT RIDERS

Sister Aimee's flair for the theatrical served her well, enabling her to do and say things that others wouldn't dare to try. A classic example was the night the Ku Klux Klan showed up at Angelus Temple in full regalia; dozens of them, massed at the back of the auditorium. A whisper, like wind through tall grasses, ran through the congregation.

The Klansmen marched down the wide aisle in perfect formation and took over the front rows. They had come, oddly enough, to honor Aimee Semple McPherson as a sterling example of "white Christianity," but Sister Aimee was having none of that. Five thousand people waited to see what she would do.

First Sister Aimee told a parable about an elderly African-American farmer who entered a beautiful church in order to worship with the congregation on a Sunday morning. The usher ordered him to leave: the church, he said in no uncertain terms, was for whites only. Outside, the heartbroken old man met a gentle stranger who comforted him: "I too have been trying to get into that church for many, many years," he said, and the old farmer "was suddenly thrilled and then comforted. For he knew deep down that he was looking into the compassionate face of Jesus . . ."[5]

Nobody spoke. Nobody moved, or coughed, or rustled a program. Sister Aimee just stood there, glaring down at the Klansmen. Then her voice rang through the auditorium:

You men who pride yourselves on patriotism, you men who have pledged yourselves to make America free for white Christianity, listen to me! Ask yourself how it is possible to pretend to worship one of the greatest Jews who ever lived, Jesus Christ, and then to despise all living Jews? I say unto you as our Master said, Judge not, that ye be not judged![6]

The Klansmen fled; not in a massed attack formation this time, but in confusion, by twos and threes. They never came to Angelus Temple again.

Given the Klan's reputation for violence, Sister Aimee had made a bold move, but she never seemed concerned about the wisdom of her actions. It was the right thing to do and she did it: end of story. She had never lacked courage; partly because that was her nature, but mostly because she believed herself to be under the protection of God.

On the stage in Angelus Temple, Sister Aimee's instinct never failed her. She knew what to do, when to do it, and just how far to go. Offstage in the real world, following her instincts plunged her headlong into scandal.

The episode began when Sister Aimee vanished while swimming at Ocean Park beach. Officials and a grieving congregation presumed that she had been drowned. Five weeks later she turned up in the Arizona desert, with an elaborate story about being kidnapped and held for ransom. A grand jury investigation into the matter disclosed no evidence of kidnapping. However, it did produce evidence to indicate that Sister Aimee had staged the whole episode in order to be with her married lover at a seaside resort in Carmel.

Though the grand jury investigation never resulted in an indictment, it produced thirty-five hundred pages of transcript; conflicting and self-contradictory testimony that damaged Sister Aimee's reputation and left her no sure way to rebuild it. At Angelus Temple she remained leader; belief in her kidnapping story became an article of faith for her congregants.

Beyond the closed world of her sanctuary, Sister Aimee lost much of her influence, but none of her notoriety. Until the end of her days, the beautiful evangelist with the whisper of scandal in her past made good copy for ambitious reporters and drew crowds of the curious to hear her preach.

Aimee Semple McPherson died on September 27, 1944.

When she lay in state at Angelus Temple, sixty thousand people came to pay their respects. Six hundred cars formed the funeral procession that took Sister Aimee to her grave in Forest Lawn Cemetery. Looking back from the standpoint of history, Sister Aimee remains an icon of the twenties. Like Babe Ruth and Texas Guinan, F. Scott Fitzgerald and Al Capone, she simply could not have happened in any other time.

The Devil and Charles Darwin

Not all leaders of the Fundamentalist movement were evangelists or ordained ministers. One of the most famous was a distinguished politician and statesman who was thrice nominated for president by the Democratic party, served as secretary of state in Woodrow Wilson's administration, and personally negotiated thirty treaties with foreign countries.

William Jennings Bryan had always been a religious man, but after his retirement from government he became increasingly active in the Fundamentalist movement and inflexibly dogmatic in his views. Defending religion against all attackers became the purpose of his life.

It was Bryan's misfortune to come up against attorney Clarence Darrow, a Jazz Age intellectual with a flair for courtroom theatrics and an irreverence that ran as deep as his opponent's grim piety. The two men met in a courtroom in Dayton, Tennessee, to argue the "Scopes monkey trial" of 1925.

The case began when the American Civil Liberties Union (ACLU) convinced high school teacher John Thomas Scopes to defy a state law that made it a crime to teach "any theory that denies the story of the Divine Creation of man as taught in the Bible."[7]

Fundamentalists of the 1920s despised the theory of evolution as a threat to everything they held dear. In the name of

Christian faith, William Jennings Bryan agreed to help the prosecution. Clarence Darrow, along with a group of ACLU attorneys, would defend John Scopes. H. L. Mencken, the journalist who once defined faith as "an illogical belief in the occurrence of the improbable,"[8] came to Dayton to cover the trial.

Both sides knew that Scopes would be found guilty. He had freely admitted to violating the law. The trial wasn't about guilt or innocence: it was about academic freedom and the seemingly irreconcilable conflicts between science and religion. Court convened on a stifling summer day, with the attorneys in shirtsleeves and the judge sitting beneath a banner that said "Read Your Bible Daily." Outside, vendors sold lemonade, hot dogs, and sandwiches; toy monkeys appeared in store windows, some for sale and some just for show.

The trial began with a victory for Bryan and the prosecution when the judge refused to allow scientists to take the stand. Their testimony would be hearsay, the judge ruled, because they could not possibly have witnessed the moment when lower animals allegedly evolved into human beings. Darrow didn't miss a beat; if he couldn't call scientists to testify as experts on science, then perhaps he could call William Jennings Bryan to testify as an expert on the Bible.

From the moment that the judge agreed and Bryan consented, it was a rout, though Bryan's talent for oratory and debate gave him a few bright moments: "You believe in the age of rocks, I believe in the Rock of Ages."[9] Darrow bedeviled the hapless Bryan with unanswerable questions: "If God is good, why does He permit pain? If the universe reveals a divine purpose, what is it? Is it immoral to learn a foreign language because, since the fall of [the Tower of Babel] God has intended that we speak different languages? How long is it since the Creation? Was Jonah really swallowed by a whale?"[10]

Bryan struggled to defend his unchanging doctrine in the

midst of a changing world, and made himself ridiculous in the process. Even the citizens of Dayton could not miss the weakness of his arguments and his abysmal lack of knowledge about science.

The trial ended more or less as everyone expected: John Scopes was found guilty and fined $100, Clarence Darrow became a hero of the Jazz Age, scientists went right on teaching Charles Darwin's theory of evolution, and Fundamentalists went right on denouncing that theory as a thing of the devil.

There was one unexpected outcome, however: broken and discredited, his beloved religion held up to ridicule, William Jennings Bryan died a few days after the trial. He was buried at Arlington National Cemetery, beneath a tombstone with a simple and eloquent inscription: "He Kept the Faith."

TEN

The Walls Come Tumblin' Down
Economic Disaster Silences the Decade That Roared

The presidential election of 1928 was officially between Democrat Al Smith and Republican Herbert Hoover, but the names listed on the ballot did not tell the whole story. These two candidates embodied the major conflicts of the Roaring Twenties: Catholic versus Protestant, wet versus dry, immigrant versus native-born, big city versus small town.

Al Smith was the son of immigrants, a scrapper from New York's lower east side. He was also an outspoken critic of prohibition and the hypocrisies surrounding it. Herbert Hoover was an Iowa-born Quaker who supported prohibition. The election turned out as predicted: with an overwhelming victory for Hoover. He dominated 21.4 million to 14 million in the popular vote, 444 to 87 in the electoral college.

Hail to the Chief

Herbert Hoover began his presidency with an outburst of activity that seemed well suited to the frantic pace of the decade. In his first six months of office he proposed tax cuts for lower income people; funded the first law school for African Americans at

Howard University; asked Congress to create a cabinet-level post for a secretary for the Department of Health, Education, and Welfare; and started the construction of Boulder Dam. In answer to the growing concern about crime in general and prohibition offenses in particular, he appointed a committee under former Attorney General George W. Wickersham to make a thorough study of prohibition and its enforcement.

Hoover didn't wait for the report from Wickersham's committee before dealing with the issue of prohibition. Politically he couldn't afford to wait; though popular support for prohibition had begun to fade, the drys were still a force in Congress. The "Jones Five and Dime Law" of 1929 made offenses against the Volstead Act into a felony, and raised maximum penalties for first-time offenders to five years in prison and a $10,000 fine, a huge sum in an era when a family of four could live on $2,000 per year.

The law was so harsh that it made prohibition even more difficult to enforce than it had been before. Hoover also appointed new federal prosecutors and raised the standards for prohibition agents.

The result of all this legislative maneuvering soon flooded the courts and the prisons with prohibition cases: many of them respectable middle class citizens who didn't take kindly to such treatment. The voices calling for repeal grew louder and more insistent. The Jones Five and Dime Law was so effective in mobilizing resistance to the Volstead Act, some historians have wondered if exactly that result hadn't been Hoover's intention all along.

"Enough, Already!"

In April 1929, Texas Guinan stood trial in federal court for selling liquor. On the day her case was scheduled, a high-spirited throng of supporters packed the courtroom and spilled over into the hallways and even into the streets. The jury ignored overwhelming evidence to vote for an acquittal, and when the verdict was announced a rousing cheer broke out in the courtroom. A brass band escorted Texas back to her club, where she threw a victory celebration that lasted for days.

Texas Guinan had been arrested before, but there was something different about this incident. This time, Texas and her boisterous entourage didn't just break the law; they defied it, they mocked it, and the jury helped them out. Given the overwhelming evidence in this case, the verdict was not a judgment of Mary Louise Guinan, but of prohibition itself.

Just before New Year's Eve, 1929, a rumrunner's vessel bringing in liquor for the upcoming holiday encountered a coast guard cutter in Narragansett Bay. When the smugglers made a break for the open sea, the crew of the cutter fired a murderous barrage, killing three of the four rumrunners. When news of the killing spread, an angry crowd of protesters descended on Boston Common and attacked a coast guard recruiter who had no personal connection to the incident.

Antiprohibition forces had always existed, but they were fragmented and largely ineffectual. They maintained a low-key, rational approach to the issue. Unfortunately, rationality isn't as dramatic as saloon-smashing, and running an organized opposition to anything is both time consuming and expensive. Most opponents of prohibition were content to break the law rather than go to all the work of changing it.

Then came 1929, the year of the Jones Five and Dime Law, the Valentine's Day massacre, and the shoot-out in Narragansett Bay. Prohibition was spinning out of control. Efforts to repeal the Eighteenth Amendment picked up steam as more people began to realize that the noble experiment had failed.

The crusade for repeal began with social and moral arguments: prohibition was breeding a whole new class of criminals, encouraging official corruption, and overcrowding the nation's prison system. All that was true enough, but in the end it wasn't principle that brought down prohibition; it was economics.

THE CRASH OF '29

On September 3, 1929, the stock market hit a new high. Then it started falling; slowly at first, then dangerously fast. By October, America plunged into the worst economic crisis in its history.

The high rollers of the Jazz Age were caught off guard by the stock market crash of October 1929. According to later economists and historians, they shouldn't have been so surprised. The signs had been there for some time; whole industries experiencing lower profits, banks making risky loans without sufficient cash reserves, and speculators throwing around margin "money" as if it was the real thing.

When the market hit the skids, brokers called for more margin (more cash) from clients who never had it in the first place: "one woman, presented by her broker with an enormous bill for more margin, cried out in bewilderment, 'How could I lose $100,000? I never *had* $100,000.'"[1]

On October 24, a wave of selling sent prices tumbling. Brokers began calling in their clients' options. Many investors didn't have the money to save their investments. The market kept slipping. Finally on October 29 the bottom fell out.

Total shares traded was 16,410,030 (at a time when five million was considered a huge day), at a loss of $15 billion. On the day of the crash, the president of Union Cigar saw his company's stock fall from $113.50 to $4.00 in a single day. Rather than face financial ruin, he jumped to his death from the window of a New York hotel. Suicide stories—and suicide jokes—became part of the legend of the crash. People laughed so they wouldn't have to cry, telling stories about pawn shops, soup lines, and hotel desk clerks asking guests if they wanted a room for sleeping—or for jumping. Prosperity vanished like fog in a midmorning sun, and the decade that roared came to a silent end.

PROHIBITION IS AN AWFUL FLOP

In the months after the crash, it wasn't just stock market speculators and big-time bankers who felt the pinch; ordinary working people who never played the market in their lives were plunged into misery.

The situation in Michigan serves as an example of the nationwide economic devastation. Unemployment soared, from a precrash level of 56,800 in September 1929 to 249,400 in December. For three years afterward, Michigan's unemployment rate averaged a whopping 34 percent, leaving thousands of families with no means of support.[2]

Antiprohibition activists seized on economic issues and transformed them into a powerful argument for repeal. Not only was prohibition expensive to enforce, it was costing the government hundreds of millions of dollars in lost revenues. Advocates of repeal contended that lost sales taxes alone could pay off the national debt, with $200 million to spare![3]

To jobless Americans who worried about feeding their families, the idea made perfect sense. Prohibition was already a travesty. The Jones Five and Dime Law had turned it into a sad, sick joke. It was time to put that joke aside and get down to the business of rebuilding the economy. A rising tide of antiprohibitionist sentiment swept through the nation. Then came the Wickersham Report.

In nineteen months the committee gathered an impressive body of evidence showing that prohibition was a failure, then inexplicably concluded that the Eighteenth Amendment should not be repealed or even modified. It deserved a further trial, they said. Nobody was in the mood to listen.

A Late and Unlamented Law

The Wickersham Report notwithstanding, it was clear that prohibition was on its way out; and so was President Hoover. The crash of 1929 derailed his presidency as surely as it wiped out the stock market. Nobody wanted Hoover anymore and nobody but a few stubborn drys wanted prohibition. With the odds turning against them, those intrepid defenders of public morals prepared once more for battle.

Andrew Volstead, the senator whose name had become synonymous with prohibition enforcement, reminded his colleagues of the evils prohibition was meant to destroy: "Do you remember the old saloon days? Do you remember the boisterous crowds inside singing songs and doing things they wouldn't do when sober? Do you remember the old barflies, those broken down men of the gutter who earned their drinks by cleaning out the spittoons and lived off the sausage and crackers on the bar?"[4]

Evangelist Billy Sunday dusted off his old prohibition sermons and went to Detroit, where he first began his crusade against demon rum. He shouted, he pranced, he thundered like he'd done back in the old days. This time, nothing felt the same. This time, the auditorium wasn't packed with people hanging onto his every word and shouting vigorous amens whenever he made a point. The crowds were sparse; older people mostly, who sat quietly with hands folded in their laps and didn't quite listen.

It was a foregone conclusion that repeal of the Eighteenth Amendment would become a plank in the 1932 Democratic platform. Franklin Delano Roosevelt, the party's charismatic nominee for president, made his position clear: "The Convention wants Repeal. I want Repeal. I am confident that the United States of America wants Repeal. I say to you now that from this day on, the Eighteenth Amendment is doomed."[5]

Roosevelt kept his word. He was inaugurated as president on March 4, 1933. On December 5, 1933, at 5:32 P.M. Eastern Standard Time, the Twenty-first Amendment became law and the Eighteenth became history. It was all very straightforward; thirteen years, ten months, and nineteen days of prohibition wiped out with a single declarative sentence: "The eighteenth article of amendment to the Constitution of the United States is hereby repealed."

And so it was over. The speakeasies closed or became legitimate night clubs. Al Capone was already in federal prison, his stranglehold on Chicago broken by the meticulous tax evasion case prepared by IRS agent Frank Wilson and U.S. attorney George E. Q. Johnson. Texas Guinan, the sassy high priestess of prohibition nightlife, died with the era she helped to define, just a few weeks before the last state ratified the Twenty-first Amendment.

Like Texas Guinan herself, the excesses of the Jazz Age were part of its quirky charm. In many ways, the Roaring Twenties finished in a decade what the Industrial Revolution (roughly 1750–1850) had taken a century to start. Both eras were marked by widespread social changes, massive shifts of population from rural to urban settings, and rapid technological advances.

During the Industrial Revolution, James Watt invented the steam engine (1769, in England), factories mass-produced items that had once been crafted by hand, railroads and steamships made travel faster and more comfortable. The resulting social changes created havoc, packing impoverished workers into grim factory towns, where they could only mourn for the simple farm life they had left behind.

During the Roaring Twenties, a generation questioned the standards of its elders. Women got the vote; prohibitionists won, then lost, their crusade against "demon rum," and the rate of technological innovation outstripped the ability of people to adjust to it. The automobile and the airplane came into their own, motion pictures and radio entertained millions, the stock market skyrocketed.

Many people wanted to believe it would never end; but of course, it did. The shaky financial underpinnings crumbled and the High Times of the 1920s gave way to the Hard Times of the 1930s. The wealthy went broke, the middle class found themselves strapped with debt for everything from automobiles to kitchen appliances, and the poor too often went homeless and hungry.

Despite all that, a generation of shieks and shebas would remember the Roaring Twenties with fondness. They had rebelled against outmoded ways and had some fun in the process. In the long and troubled annals of human history that's not a bad achievement.

SOURCE NOTES

INTRODUCTION

1. F. Scott Fitzgerald, in Time-Life Books, *This Fabulous Century: 1920–1930* (New York: Time-Life Books, 1988), 4.

ONE

1. Bernard Weisberger, "A Nation of Immigrants," *American Heritage* (Feb./March 1994): 84.

2. Ibid.

3. Geoffrey Perrett, *America in the Twenties: A History* (New York: Simon and Schuster, 1982), 167.

4. Larry Engelmann, *Intemperance: The Lost War Against Liquor* (New York: The Free Press, 1979), 15.

5. Pledge of the Woman's Christian Temperance Union, in Emmet G. Coleman, ed., *The Temperance Songbook* (New York: American Heritage Press, 1971), 79.

6. William Allen White, in Engelmann, *Intemperance*, 30.

7. Ring Lardner, in Engelmann, 30.

TWO

1. Time-Life Books, *This Fabulous Century*, 36.

2. Engelmann, *Intemperance*, 77.

3. Ernest R. May, *The Life History of the United States: Vol. 10: Boom and Bust* (New York: Time-Life Books, 1974), 51–53.

4. Moe Smith, in May, *The Life History of the United States*, 52.

5. Henry B. Joy, in Engelmann, *Intemperance*, 103.

THREE

1. Time-Life Books, *This Fabulous Century*, 62.

2. F. Scott Fitzgerald, in John A. Garraty, *The American Nation* (New York: HarperCollins College Publishers, 1995). In *Multimedia U.S. History: The Story of a Nation* (Parsippany, N.J.: Bureau of Electronic Publishing, 1994), Chapter 25, n.p.

3. Time-Life Books, *This Fabulous Century*, 60.

4. Marc McCutcheon, *The Writer's Guide to Everyday Life from Prohibition through World War II* (Cincinnati, Ohio: Writer's Digest Books, 1995), 85–88.

5. Time-Life Books, *This Fabulous Century*, 24.

6. Ned Jordan, "Somewhere West of Laramie," in *This Fabulous Century*, 25.

FOUR

1. Herbert Ashbury, *The Great Illusion*, in Perrett, *America in the Twenties*, 177.

2. David Levering Lewis, ed., *The Portable Harlem Renaissance Reader* (New York: Penguin Books, 1994), xxii.

3. Langston Hughes, in Lewis, *The Portable Harlem Renaissance Reader*, 78.

4. Perrett, *America in the Twenties*, 233.

5. Louis Adamic, in Kevin Starr, *Material Dreams: Southern California Through the 1920s* (New York: Oxford University Press, 1990), 132.

6. Ibid.

7. Starr, 170.

FIVE

1. Laurence Bergreen, *Capone: The Man and the Era* (New York: Simon and Schuster, 1994), 367.

2. Jack Kelly, "Gangster City," *American Heritage* (April 1995): 66.

3. Colonel Henry Barrett Chamberlin, in Bergreen, *Al Capone*, 86.

4. Bergreen, 130.

SIX

1. Warren G. Harding, in Perrett, *America in the Twenties*, 116.

2. May, *The Life History of the United States*, 65.

3. Perrett, *America in the Twenties*, 112.

4. Alice Roosevelt Longworth, in May, *The Life History of the United States*, 67.

5. Perrett, *America in the Twenties*, 135–136.

6. William Z. Ripley, in Perrett, 286.

7. T. H. Watkins, *The Great Depression: America in the 1930s* (Boston: Little, Brown and Co., 1993), 38.

8. Ibid., 39.

9. May, 131.

SEVEN

1. Divine, Robert A., T. J. Breen, George M. Fredrickson, and R. Hal Williams, *America: Past and Present* (New York: HarperCollins College Publishers, 1995). In *Multimedia U.S. History*, Chapter 25, n.p.

2. Orville Dewey, in Donald O. Bolander, ed., *Instant Quotation Dictionary* (Mundelein, Illinois: Career Institute, 1972), 165.

3. Divine, n.p.

4. Charles Rumford Walker, in Perrett, *America in the Twenties*, 42.

5. Kenneth C. Davis, *Don't Know Much About History* (New York: Crown Publishers, Inc., 1990). In *Multimedia U.S. History*, Chapter 6, n.p.

6. Ibid.

7. Bartolomeo Vanzetti, letter to his son, April 9, 1927, in George Seldes, ed., *The Great Thoughts* (New York: Ballantine Books, 1985), 429.

EIGHT

1. Materials on the "Palmer sisters" are drawn from family records and the author's memory. The names and some nonmaterial details have been changed to protect the family's privacy. None of the three

sisters are still alive in 1997, but numerous children, grandchildren, and great-grandchildren are scattered throughout the United States.

2. *Christian Evangelist*, Dec. 13, 1923, in Stanley Coben, *Rebellion Against Victorianism* (New York: Oxford University Press, 1991), 147.

NINE

1. May, *The Life History of the United States*, 112.

2. Lyle W. Dorsett, *Billy Sunday and the Redemption of Urban America* (Grand Rapids, Michigan: William B. Eerdmans Publishing Co., 1991), 113.

3. Billy Sunday, in Lyle W. Dorsett, 70.

4. Billy Sunday, in May, *The Life History of the United States*, 94.

5. Aimee Semple McPherson, in Epstein, *Sister Aimee* (New York: Harcourt Brace Jovanovich, 1993), 262.

6. Ibid., 263.

7. Quoted in Garraty, *The American Nation*. In *Multimedia U. S. History*, Chapter 25, n.p.

8. H. L. Mencken, in Seldes, *The Great Thoughts*, 282.

9. Perrett, *America in the Twenties*, 201.

10. Kevin Tierney, *Darrow: A Biography* (New York: Thomas Y. Crowell, 1979), 366.

TEN

1. Time-Life Books, *This Fabulous Century*, 20.

2. Engelmann, *Intemperance*, 198.

3. Ibid., 199.

4. Andrew Volstead, in Engelmann, 1.

5. Franklin D. Roosevelt, in Engelmann, 188.

FURTHER READING

Brownlow, Kevin, and John Kobal. *Hollywood: The Pioneers*. New York: Alfred A. Knopf, 1979.

Chalmers, David M. *Hooded Americanism: The History of the Ku Klux Klan*. New York: New Viewpoints, 1976.

Commager, Henry Steele, ed. *The American Destiny*. Vol. 13, *The Twenties*. New York: Danbury Press, 1976.

Darrow, Clarence. *The Story of My Life*. New York: Charles Scribner's Sons, 1932.

Drew, William M. *Speaking of Silents: First Ladies of the Screen*. New York: Vestal Press, 1979.

Pfeffer, Paula F. A. *Philip Randolph, Pioneer of the Civil Rights Movement*. Baton Rouge, Lou.: Louisiana State University Press, 1990.

Starr, Kevin. *Inventing the Dream: California Through the Progressive Era*. New York: Oxford University Press, 1985.

ABOUT THE AUTHOR

Linda Jacobs Altman specializes in writing about history, social issues, and multicultural subjects for young people. Her titles include *Genocide: The Systematic Killing of a People* and *Amelia's Road,* the story of a young Mexican-American migrant farmworker and her search for a home. Altman is a member of the Society of Children's Book Writers and Illustrators and the National Storytelling Association.

Mrs. Altman and her husband live off a dirt road in Clearlake, California. They are movie nuts with an ever-growing video collection, Forty-Niner fans who never miss a televised game, and surrogate parents to four cats, three dogs, and a pair of cockatiels.